Studying Abroad/
Learning Abroad

STUDYING ABROAD/
LEARNING ABROAD

(AN ABRIDGED EDITION OF
THE WHOLE WORLD GUIDE
TO CULTURE LEARNING)

J. Daniel Hess

INTERCULTURAL PRESS, INC.

For information, contact:
Intercultural Press, Inc.
PO Box 700
Yarmouth, Maine 04096 USA
207-846-5168
www.interculturalpress.com

Book design by Patty J. Topel
Production by Lisa Michelsen Golden
Original cover design by Lois Leonard Stock

Printed in the United States of Americas

05 04 03 02 01 00   3 4 5 6 7 8

Library of Congress Cataloging-in-Publication Data

Hess, J. Daniel. (John Daniel), 1937-
     Studying abroad/learning abroad : an abridged version of The whole world guide to culture learning / J. Daniel Hess.
     p.   cm.
     Includes bibliographical references. (p.).
     ISBN 1-877864-50-1
1. Foreign study. 2. American students—Foreign countries. 3. International education. 4. Experiential learning. 5. Returned students—United States. I. Hess, J. Daniel. (John Daniel), 1937- Whole world guide to culture learning. II. Title.

LB2375.H467 1997
370.116—dc21   97-11428
                                                              CIP

Table of Contents

Preface

Three years into my teaching career, we (my family and I) were invited by Goshen College to open a study-service program in Costa Rica. Our innocent acceptance of the assignment fundamentally changed the boundaries of both my career definition and my cultural orientation. In the following twenty-five years, we directed thirteen trimesters of study service in Costa Rica. As we helped our students attain their goals, we, too, became culture learners. Gradually, my orientation became multicultural, and the territory of studies that I called my specialty came to include the large field of intercultural communication.

I don't regret the redirection into cross-cultural studies, nor the movement from ethnocentricity toward multiculturalism. The social, intellectual, emotional, and spiritual rewards have been many—including the privilege of writing this book.

The seeds were sown in Costa Rica in social interactions

with friends and neighbors, in our acculturation into "Tico" life, and in the discussions and activities that made up the study-service curriculum. Residencies and visits to other places in Central America, Spain, and Thailand, along with our coming into contact with the vast literature of intercultural communication, nurtured our culture learning.

Throughout the days of writing and revising, I've been grateful for the many witnesses to this work, people who not only surrounded me, but spoke into the text a word or sentence or chapter.

The first and most important ones are those who have shared friendship with us overseas. Mima and Juan Vianey, Doris and Jorge, Zenón and Lilia, Humberto, Ellie, Sonia, Edwin, Rodrigo, Flor, Maylie and Alfonso, Jaime and Lali, Paco and Pilar, Corrine, and many, many others.

And those who, upon introducing and interpreting their culture to us, demonstrated the discipline and compassion of humane world citizens: Henry Paul and Mildred Yoder in Cuba; Vernon and Dottie Jantzi in Nicaragua; in Honduras, Amzie Yoder and, later, Linda Shelly; and Aulden Coble and Dave Kaufman in Costa Rica. Included in this listing are people who worked with refugees, such as Henry Neufeld in Thailand and Mabel Paetkau in Canada.

Goshen College is imprinted deeply into these pages: the international students on campus; the 250 students who learned with us in Costa Rica; the Goshen College faculty who led similar study-service units across the globe; the Goshen College International Education Office and, specifically, Ruth Gunden; the early leaders in Goshen's international program including Henry Weaver, Paul Mininger, Arlin Hunsberger, and J. Lawrence Burkholder; and colleagues in the English and Communication departments.

How can one adequately thank the community of scholars who comprise the bibliography at the end of this book and those others whose ideas were informally handed down from person to person and unknowingly used here? Among the names who have shaped my understanding of intercultural communication are Margaret Mead, Edward T. Hall, Eugene B. Nida, Marshall R. Singer, Larry A. Samovar and Richard E. Porter, John C. Condon, William B. Gudykunst and Young Yun Kim, and Dean C. Barnlund.

My work takes place in community. In Goshen the Becks,

Hertzlers, and Yoders are my center of reference. In Chapel Hill and Raleigh, "The Weekenders" include the Boos family, the Bushes (Greg, Jon, Eric, and Pam) and the North-Martins. The Indiana Consortium for International Programs provided some financial assistance for an earlier version.

Mennonite Central Committee, no matter where it's located on the globe with its program, points true north.

David S. Hoopes and his colleagues at Intercultural Press deserve the highest commendation for knowledge of the subject, editorial coaching, and professional collegiality. And thanks to my family, each of whom models for me how to be a culture learner.

Introduction

Most people who go abroad encounter things about their host culture which disturb them. Reaction to these aspects of the culture can sometimes color their entire experience in the country and turn it grey. To adapt satisfactorily and to effectively exploit the opportunities for culture learning, it is necessary to face the challenges of overcoming negative responses that are so prevalent among people moving into a new culture. One of the best ways to overcome these negative responses is to name them, look them in the face, and come to terms with that which cannot be changed. That is what this book is about—facing squarely the difficulties inherent in cross-cultural experience so that the sojourner can reap the rewards in culture learning.

Let's start with you. You might be a student enrolled in an American college or university who wants to spend an academic year abroad. Perhaps you're just taking a short vacation trip to Mexico. Or you've volunteered to work with a nongovernmental organization for three years in East Africa or are going to teach English in Thailand. Maybe you're a missionary nurse headed for Bolivia, or you're a volunteer social worker in India.

Whether you sling on a backpack and go vagabonding, set off with your family on a corporate assignment abroad, or register to study in a national university, you probably aren't the type who'll be content to live in the North American ghetto in the foreign city, sleep every day till noon, drown out the world with your boombox and favorite CDs from back home. Whatever your motivation for going abroad, I suspect that you will want to devote yourself to the serious task of learning another culture, developing relationships with the people you meet, communicating effectively, and adapting to the environment so as to make your time abroad as enjoyable and productive as possible.

Having said all this, it is our expectation that this book will be especially valuable to students who are going on their own or with organized study abroad programs. The methods addressed here rely heavily on experiential learning as practiced and valued at both the college and secondary levels. It calls for the intellectual discipline demanded of students in a more or less structured educational environment. It expects its users to be ready to adopt an inquiring frame of mind which characterizes all good students.

This book is directed toward students and students come in all ages, shapes and sizes. Thus, if you have an inquiring mind, this book ought to go along with you, even if you travel light.

Culture Learning

This book is dedicated to helping sojourners communicate across cultures. Not all travelers come naturally to culture learning. Not all who travel to and reside in foreign countries, even those who remain for five, ten, or more years, take on the task of comprehending the way of life of their hosts. To be sure, most people who leave home for an international trip bring home stories of their adventures and descriptions of the people they saw. Some may talk about the quaint habits, the new foods, and strange costumes encountered along the way. They show their snapshots and purchases. But this booty doesn't confirm that culture learning has taken place. For many, the gap between their native culture and the foreign culture remains unbridged. "East is East and West is West and never the twain shall meet," said Rudyard Kipling. In the twentieth century, a science-oriented communication specialist has proclaimed: "There is no such thing as cross-cultural communication" (Martin 1976). These words sound scary, as do the attitudes they reflect.

To counter the possibilities of cultural separation, alienation, and even hostility that stem from such attitudes, we argue in these pages for the value of culture learning and the significance of intercultural communication. It is our intent to help each reader become what Eric J. Leed (1991, 2) calls "the brokers of contacts" among cultures—that is, people who not only know how to study cultures but also how to move comfortably from one culture to another and how to help other sojourners to bridge cultural gaps.

What is culture learning? Who does it? When? How? Why should a person want to engage in culture learning? What is the result of culture learning?

Chapter 1 serves as a general tour of the subject of culture learning. It introduces crucial concepts and prepares you to follow the discussions and to use the guides which follow.

What is culture?

Culture learning has to do with (1) culture, (2) learners, and (3) a learning process. We'll begin with culture. It's a bit difficult to define precisely, but here's a definition you may find useful:

> Culture is the sum total of ways of living, including values, beliefs, esthetic standards, linguistic expression, patterns of thinking, behavioral norms, and styles of communication which a group of people has developed to assure its survival in a particular physical and human environment. Culture and the people who are part of it interact so that culture is not static. Culture is the response of a group of human beings to the valid and particular needs of its members. It, therefore, has an inherent logic and an essential balance between positive and negative dimensions (Hoopes 1979, 3).

You may think of culture as the subject matter of culture learning in the same way that plant life is the subject matter of botany—or poetry the subject matter of literature. However, culture as "something to be learned" is a little difficult to get your mind around. On a continuum ranging from fluff stuff to the killers (students know how to rank their courses), the content of culture learning places among the more demanding of the disciplines. The reason for the difficulty is not that there's a lot to memorize, but rather that the material is elusive. Not only are people generally unaware of their own culture (they take it for granted), but they are also outsiders to the other's culture, naive and innocent of what the natives take for granted.

Four years after the end of the so-called Cultural Revolution in the People's Republic of China, I tried to teach a group of Chinese professors about culture and its influence on human behavior. The biggest challenge of that course was to come to a common understanding of the concept of culture. Although they spoke of their own cultural revolution (which was hard for me to fathom), the sense of culture as an indigenous and dynamic way of being seemed a strange idea to them. The word culture is frequently used, but its significance often hides itself from people.

Culture learning and cross-cultural adaptation

Culture learning can be seen as part of the process of cross-cultural adaptation that people experience when they go abroad to live. The study of this subject goes back to work done by Sverre Lysgaard (1955) and John Taylor and Jeanne E. Gullahorn (1963) in which the theory of the U curve—and subsequently the W curve—of cross-cultural adjustment was formulated.

The U-curve theory was based on the observation that most people when they live for some time in a foreign country go through a series of transition stages that, when graphed, form the shape of a U. They start out in a state of excitement and interest (often called euphoria), begin to experience difficulties in functioning in the culture, reach a nadir of dissatisfaction and discontent, and then begin to pull out of it, until they finally reestablish a stable emotional state of being. The W curve (literally "double U") was suggested by the fact that when long-term sojourners return home they go through a similar kind of reentry adjustment.

This process is also referred to as culture shock, especially when the bottom of the adjustment cycle (or U curve) is reached. The principal cause of culture shock lies in the encounter with differences—but not just the exotic differences of the immediate senses, the sights, sounds, and smells of the new environment. It is the differences in the way the society is organized and in the values, behaviors, styles of communication, and patterns of thinking that cause the problem, since so much of what makes up these basic cultural characteristics is automatic and unconscious and is assumed to be universal. When we encounter differences in these basic ways of being, we are thrown off without knowing why. Things mean something different from what we expect. Our behaviors are misunderstood. Our sense of who we are becomes confused. The cues by which we govern our behavior and identify ourselves at home are gone or mean something different. At the simplest level, a gesture which to you means "OK" may in another culture, Brazil, for instance, be an obscenity. At a deeper level, you may instinctively avoid political arguments with people outside your family and be offended when a Dane challenges you on political issues. Or you may solve problems by using information and instruments you have, where a Frenchperson would think you shallow if you didn't start with a clear theoretical framework.

The reaction to culture shock varies from person to person but may consist of such things as irritability, depression, loss of sleep or appetite (or, conversely, compensations such as overeating), anger, loss of self-esteem, and others. It may result in the person wanting to go (or sometimes actually going) home or developing a very hostile stance toward everything about the host culture. The emergence from this stage of culture shock occurs as you *learn* the host culture. As the values which your hosts live by become more identifiable and appear more reasonable, as the customs and expected behaviors become familiar and you can engage in them comfortably and in a manner which gets the response you want, the emotional effects of culture shock begin to dissipate. The cues become decipherable; you can interpret and predict what is happening or going to happen around you. You feel better about yourself and your hosts. (For more on culture shock, see Guide 7.)

Culture learning and cross-cultural adjustment are therefore closely linked in the experience of the person living abroad. The pursuit of culture learning speeds you along the road to effective cross-cultural adaptation. The pursuit of effective adaptation provides the context and content for culture learning.

The culture-learning continuum

A number of scholars have suggested that there is a culture-learning continuum along which people can be seen to progress. Most of these continua show a movement from ethnocentrism to some form of multiculturalism. They are useful in enabling you to identify where you and/or others are located in the stages of development and growth described. One of the most interesting and useful models has been proposed by Milton J. Bennett and is called "A Developmental Model of Intercultural Sensitivity" (1993).

In Bennett's model, the progress of an individual from ethnocentrism to what he refers to as "ethnorelativism" depends on how she or he deals with cultural differences, which in turn defines the level the person is at in the developmental process. Bennett identifies six stages in that process:

1. Ethnocentrism—a simple denial that the differences exist. The pure ethnocentric believes that the whole world is like him or her, but pure ethnocentrism is a rarely found state of being.

2. Defensiveness—the perception that the differences one encounters are threatening. Barriers are raised and negative judgments made against those who are different.

3. Minimization of the perceived differences—the perception that the differences are not very great or very important. "We're all alike under the skin," is the minimalist's rubric.

4. Acceptance—the recognition that differences exist, that they are substantial and important, and that they can be both positive and negative.

5. Adaptation—the willingness to accommodate and adjust one's behavior to the patterns and styles of another culture.

6. Adoption and integration—the merging of selected aspects of another culture into one's own cultural iden-

tity or patterns of thinking and behaving, leading to one's becoming a bi- or multicultural person.

Successful culture learners inevitably push themselves along this continuum, although their progress is rarely without setbacks. Identifying where you stand on it can give you an indication of the degree of progress you are making in your culture-learning endeavors.

Peter Adler, in his seminal writings on cultural identity (1974, 1975, 1977), elaborated on the final stage of the culture-learning continuum. The passage through culture shock and cross-cultural adaptation, Adler suggests, is accompanied by a stressful challenge to and change in the identity of the sojourner. But the sense of isolation and questioning of self that results from the experience is not to be seen as a call to despair. It is instead a springboard for the creation or evolution of a new identity which is "inclusive of life patterns different from [one's] own....We can call this new type of person multicultural because he [or she] embodies a core process of self-verification that is grounded in both the universality of the human condition and the diversity of cultural forms" (1977, 157).

But what do these abstractions about cross-cultural learning and identity mean in practical terms for the culture learner? They do not suggest, nor do we recommend, that you engage in morbid introspection throughout the time of your travel or residence in another culture, but rather they indicate the need for a regular and careful processing of the stuff of culture as one undoes and resets the culture boundaries in the mind and heart. You may and should ask, what are the components of this culture that you are using to shape who you are?

Culture learning and communication

One of the processes to which every learner must give attention is intercultural communication, which involves much more than learning and speaking a foreign language.

Edward T. Hall, in his classic study, *The Silent Language* (1981), to which we will refer again in another context, argued succinctly that "culture is communication," meaning that all the ways of behaving, thinking, valuing, and organizing within the context of a culture are special to that culture and communicate something about it. They constitute a "silent language" or what is sometimes referred to as the cultural code. Here we focus particularly on nonverbal communication, but with a meaning much broader than gestures and physical expressions.

When you enter a cultural environment different from your own, you encounter a whole new communication system. Even if you know or understand the language, there are many ways people communicate with each other and give meanings to behavior which are special to that culture. They may laugh when they are unhappy; body odors may be valued; touching, taboo; privacy, disrespected; dependency on others, a virtue. While not much will be absolutely unique, these cultural characteristics will exist in different combinations and intensities and, at the deepest level, will be anywhere from significantly to radically different from your own.

The basic problem lies in the fact that in your own society when you attempt to communicate with someone, there is a broad base of shared cultural experience—values, customary behaviors, ways of thinking and perceiving—that provides the context for the message. This base enables each of you engaged in the process of sending messages back and forth to interpret what you see and hear in very nearly the same way. At the simplest level, if an American is chatting with a passing acquaintance and one of them ends the conversation by saying, "Let's get together sometime," each one understands there is no obligation to do so—and in most cases not even an expectation that it will occur. The foreign student in the United States frequently expects the getting together to take place, because he or she doesn't understand American communication styles and patterns of personal relations.

At a more complex level, culture defines the obligations people in the society have toward each other. In many, there are elaborate rituals of reciprocity in giving gifts or paying the bill on social occasions. Americans tend to be wary of and avoid social obligations of this sort and the personal entanglements they involve. Because of the value placed by American culture on independence and self-sufficiency, Americans are more likely to want to pay their own way.

While at a distance these kinds of differences may not seem so problematic, when they are multiplied by all the dimensions of culture and when you are in the midst of them and in a state of confusion, they can scuttle your best efforts to communicate effectively.

Even if people speak the same language, as, for instance, the Americans, Australians, and British do, beneath the linguistic surface each finds the other very different in the assumptions they make about life, in the values they hold dear, in their behavior patterns and ways of thinking—so much so that they are often amazed at the conflict and disagreement which occur in cross-cultural encounters. Australians, for instance, suppress recognition of outstanding individual achievement while Americans glorify it. When Australians start cutting Americans down to size, watch out.

In a country where the language is foreign to you, even if you speak it—unless you learned it as a child growing up in that country—there will be major dimensions of the culture you will not understand. There will be nonverbal cues you will not pick up until you have been there a long time or study systematically as a culture learner.

It is important then for the overseas sojourner to recognize that there is a cultural code as well as a linguistic code to be learned and that the more attention given to learning it and the more rapidly it is learned, the quicker the person will progress along the culture-learning and cross-cultural adaptation paths. (Guides 2 and 3 address communication issues.)

Culture learning and values

There are two major dimensions to the values question in the culture-learning experience. One relates to the fundamental role of assumptions, values, and worldviews in determining the cultural patterns the stranger encounters. The other involves the question of value relativity: how can you be clear about values and ethics when your basic ideas of right and wrong differ significantly from those of your hosts?

The latter question will be dealt with extensively in chapter 5. Here we will examine how values affect the practical pursuit of knowledge in a foreign culture. Our assumptions about the world and the values by which we decide what is right and wrong, good and bad, are buried deeply within us. They were put there over the long period of time we were children and were acculturated into the society of our family, friends, neighbors, teachers, mentors, and other important people in our lives. They are believed and followed so instinctively that most of the time they are out of awareness. In fact, the nearer one is to the ethnocentric end of the culture-learning spectrum the more one will assume that one's own values are natural and universal.

Even for those who accept the proposition that other cultures have different values, it is still a shock to discover how many and how significant the differences are.

The reason for the inescapability of this cross-cultural surprise is that it is difficult to be aware of the values that govern our lives until they are contrasted with different ones, until we are removed from the environment in which they are "natural." It is like not realizing how necessary oxygen is to our survival until we are deprived of it.

To give a specific example, many Americans have no idea that the kind of individualism valued by Americans is, in many cultures, valued very little, and in some is actually considered a negative trait. Many have no idea that American concepts of personal privacy and private property are not held by people in a number of other countries. Many have no idea that what one personally achieves is in some countries valued much less than one's social status or family connections.

Students of intercultural relations have called these values and beliefs "cultural baggage," which we carry with us everywhere we go but without realizing we have it. We'll come back to cultural baggage later.

The point is that the culture learner must be ready to encounter differences in very important values when she or he goes abroad, and must be willing to suspend judgment and observe the nature and significance of the differences before reacting within a right/wrong, good/bad framework. (See Guides 8 and 9 for exercises in exploring values, both one's own and those of others.)

The process of culture learning

Culture learning is the effort to gain insight into how cultural strangers live. That means, of course, that one must do more than memorize a few key words of their vocabulary or mimic a few of their interesting behaviors; it involves much more than just hanging around until you catch on. Rather, one must come to know the basics of the culture—the

worldviews, values, ways of thinking, styles of communication, and patterns of behavior that are shared. In the Philippines, for example, that may mean learning the complex values embedded in the concept of harmony in human relationships: *Pakikisama*, getting along with others; *Hiya*, maintaining self-respect, having and saving "face," and fearing shame;
and *Utang na loob*, the balancing of obligations and debts
(Gochenour 1990). Each culture one attempts to learn offers
mysteries of this kind that must be understood.

Culture learning, when done properly, calls for cognitive,
affective, and behavioral knowing. Cognitive learning is typically associated with traditional classroom mastery of a subject through conventional intellectual discipline. The subject matter might include the theory of culture, a description
of people and their customs, and analyses of cultural differences. For example, one may study the Japanese use of the
go-between, or mediator, in situations of social negotiations.
The concept may be introduced, described, and illustrated
by a teacher. Typically this type of instruction and learning
takes place in a classroom setting.

Affective learning is of a different kind. Mildred Sikkema
and Agnes Niyekawa talk about affective learning in terms of
active rather than passive understanding, "the development
at gut level of an attitude of acceptance, respect, and tolerance of cultural differences" (1987, 4). In learning affectively
about the Japanese tradition of the go-between, one not only
describes and defines it intellectually, one has an emotional
response to the experience and feels the subtlety of the role
played by the go-between and its importance in maintaining
the social harmony which the Japanese value as much as, if
not more than, the Filipinos.

Behavioral learning presents an equal challenge—to learn
so well that one lives differently than one did before as a
monocultural or ethnocentric person. Ultimately, the learner
begins to behave in ways that save face in the Philippines,
or, if in Japan, he or she calls upon a go-between at just the
right moment. All education should have such transforming
behavioral effects. We all know, however, that straight A's in
exams at school do not necessarily predict how one lives
after graduation. So it is that culture learning isn't completed
until the learner is transformed.

You should not be surprised, then, that the most effective and efficient culture learning takes place not in the class-room, but on-site—in a store, on the job, at a host family's dinner table, in an intersection where people of differing cultures bump into each other. It takes place in various social situations where you encounter people behaving in the normal context of their culture. Thus, obviously, you can best learn about Brazil in Brazil. The way to learn about kibbutzim is to go live and work on a kibbutz. The term used in this manual to describe this type of on-site learning is the *action-reflection-response strategy*. In brief, this strategy is a tool to help turn ordinary (and sometimes extraordinary) events of life into instructional modules. You teach yourself using your own experiences in the foreign setting.

The dynamics of culture learning

Recently a friend of mine went overseas for a year. As expected, she suffered culture shock. But the letters she wrote to me (and others) while she was there indicate that she will be numbered among culture learners. As you read several excerpts from these letters, notice how she shifts from newcomer to a committed learner. The first excerpt is lifted from a passage about how tough the initial month was.

> I miss desperately the people and activities left behind; I'm moody and cry easily; frustrated with situations (family, neighborhood, university) that don't suit me, I begin to think about and question my aspirations, my goals.

Her candid confession, arising from the painfulness of culture shock, is understandably focused upon herself. And then within two weeks comes another letter that shows a shifting of her focus that surely must have required extraordinary effort.

> In the next six weeks I'm going to be doing intensive language study—writing, reading and I'll be translating either a book or some articles. I see writing in this language as transportation to get to other options—I'm looking forward to ecology studies, for example. (Also nutrition, art and literature.) I need this year— all of it: the immersion into a culture that now

11

intrigues me even more, the introduction to a world of emotions I'd never felt before....

She will become a culture learner through her language and ecology studies and through her interests in the specific subjects she lists, but equally important, she will become a culture learner through gradually coming to terms with and understanding the emotions she is experiencing. This learning will not occur through passive endurance but through an active investment of herself.

Culture learning, then, is not only a prescription for overcoming culture shock, but a process of growth and transformation. Whereas some people go home early and others build a wall to keep out the host culture, and still others make grudging accommodations to the strange customs, the successful culture learner commits to a journey from a monocultural beginning point to a larger world in which he or she develops new perspectives, learns new mental, emotional, and behavioral responses, and builds intercultural bridges— in short, becomes a new cultural person.

All of this is easier said than done. A culture is a powerful force, created over a long period of time for its own members. A culture is contained and coherent, with its own internal logic and unspoken laws. It is dynamic. Its energy is capable of thwarting you or of making your culture learning an exciting passage.

Chapter 2

Attitudes and Character Traits That Promote Culture Learning

Attitudes

Whether you succeed in bridging the chasm that separates cultures and that Kipling found so striking depends largely on the kind of sojourner you choose to be. What is the difference between those who effect a meeting of cultures and those who do not?

J. Lawrence Burkholder, who flew relief supplies into China during its civil war in the late 1940s and later became a professor at Harvard and then president of Goshen College, has characterized the curious traveler as "one of the most delightful persons of Western civilization," but he hastens to distinguish these "Marco Polos" of the Western world from the self-centered modern tourist. The traditional traveler, according to Burkholder, "learned new customs, ate strange foods and met different races, heard legends, observed religious customs and formed deep friendships.... The traveler said, in effect, 'I want to know you and your culture because you have something to offer me and my people'." In contrast, the tourist "adopts a quick, packaged schedule, makes a standardized trip, lives out of suitcases, observes historical monuments, and collects souvenirs. The tourist stops, snaps pictures, and defends his or her pocketbook" (Showalter 1989, 27-28).

Similar is the executive who stops to do business in six cities in five days and experiences the world only in the rarefied atmosphere of first-class plane cabins, high-priced hotel rooms, and expensive restaurants. Burkholder calls on us all to be travelers of high quality rather than self-centered tourists on a junket.

As noted in the last chapter, all travelers carry cultural baggage—a set of assumptions, values, attitudes, and behaviors that may slip through customs checks unobserved and accompany them everywhere they go on their journey. These attitudes are their intellectual and emotional apparel. Unlike the contents of their luggage, however, this cultural baggage is rarely taken out and examined, seldom altered to fit the different conditions encountered in their travels, and rarely evaluated to see if it is appropriate or adapted to what they are doing.

You will find described here four attitudes that go a long way toward ensuring success in your cross-cultural travels and interactions. They are (1) a high regard for culture, (2) an eagerness to learn, (3) a desire to make connections, and (4) a readiness to give as well as receive.

A high regard for culture

The first attitude has to do with how you regard culture. Do you have a high regard for culture or a low one? The person with a low regard for culture perceives cultural differences as a social handicap to be gotten rid of. Several years ago in an orientation class for a group going to three countries (coincidentally all beginning with *B*—Bangladesh, Bolivia, and Burkina Faso), the participants discussed their participation in a weekend of educational service in an inner-city ghetto.

14

They closed the session with prayers, during which one person asked God to "make culture as nothing, so that we can love and serve." The prayer suggested that cultural differences were an impediment to their good intentions.

A person with a high regard for culture, on the other hand, sees the diversity of peoples on the earth as good and the social dynamic that produces that diversity as a valuable and productive force.

Venturing into foreign cultures and among strangers is seen as an opportunity to comprehend the wide diversity in human existence and to find new options for human relationships.

An eagerness to learn

A second attitude pertains to your feelings about change. Do you want, during your travels, to remain stable and fixed, preserving what now is, or do you want to be changed by the experience? A cross-cultural setting can be a violent tidal wave that you brace yourself against or it can be a classroom of first rank. There, in a context that takes away the familiar props that help you preserve your routines, something extraordinary occurs. You are jolted, sometimes shocked, given unfamiliar cues, forced onto unknown paths. The newness, the strangeness, the unpleasantness—it is often unpleasant—arouse unfamiliar feelings. You find that your old ideas don't work. Things are not what they seem to be.

The traveler who welcomes this kind of challenge in hopes of learning new facts, gaining new understandings, changing old opinions, shaping new interpretations, and making new commitments is, in those very acts, positioning himself or herself to learn.

Many illustrations could be given. Sojourners with a mind to learn discover the importance of knowing what Taoism is, which are the South African writers of note, who the Shiites are, where European surveyors drew boundaries for Arab peoples, why the Shining Path is attacking foreigners in Peru, and what "magic realism" is. They may want to learn the crafts of a country, understand better how the legal system works, or explore the subtleties of negotiating or bargaining in a different cultural context. Given a curriculum of this social dimension, the person who embarks on culture learning can never return home the same, for the impact of the "textbook" in this course is to redefine the boundaries of personal commitment forever.

A desire to make connections

A third attitude to be recommended for the effective sojourner is the desire to make connections. Here's an example of two different kinds of traveler: one stays close to the travel group and moves around only in the tourist bus, never venturing out of sight of the tour leader; the other is at the edge of the group, taking early morning walks, trying to talk with the shopkeepers, and using a free afternoon to travel independently to an archeological site in order to find out how the diggers do their work.

Compare two kinds of Americans living abroad: one lives in an American enclave, buys food at an American commissary or where the storekeeper speaks English, attends American social and cultural events, and reads books and magazines from the States. The other moves in with a local family for the first few months in order to learn the language, attends wild Tuesday night soccer matches, sitting in the section of bleachers where the die-hard fans congregate, and drinks coffee regularly in the local cafe.

These descriptions highlight the differences in association patterns. While I don't agree with L. John Martin, who, as noted before, says that "there is no such thing as cross-cultural communication" (1976), it is certainly clear that travelers who remain totally isolated from the people of the host culture, ignorant of their customs, and bent on defending the sanctity of their own cultural norms, will find communication difficult. Intercultural living *is* a risky proposition. Not all the natives are perfect hosts, nor are all travelers friendly guests. Not all merchants are honest, and not all cultural characteristics are benign. When strangers discover that the cultural chasm is deep and wide, not all of them have the will to persevere nor the skills to build bridges and find common cultural ground. Sometimes, even with the best of efforts, communication breaks down, culture shock sets in more or less permanently, and people become enemies. If two people are totally estranged, there can be no communication. If, on the other hand, the partners in communication work hard to establish a common ground of some sort and make the effort to form a connection, they will succeed in creating their own unique common culture. The second person described in each of the examples at the beginning of this section is forming the associations necessary for culture learning.

A readiness to give as well as receive

The fourth attitude for the effective traveler is a meaningful sense of reciprocity and the willingness to engage in mutual or cooperative interchange.

Travel, by its nature, tends to be self-serving. One makes a trip in order to have fun, to see the world, to satisfy curiosity, to make money, to escape responsibility, to earn college credits, to be with one's spouse, or to seek a better life. One returns home with advantages for having traveled.

It's a lot to ask such a traveler to try to associate with foreigners, to build a common cultural ground, to make the first attempts at communication. It's asking even more to propose that as a traveler you set up exchanges with strangers and arrangements for sharing that enrich both parties so that other people benefit as much as you do from your travel.

However idealistic this may sound, people who display the imagination to locate opportunities for interacting with strangers, the courage to make the first moves, the graciousness to begin receiving what the strangers have to offer, the resourcefulness to give of themselves to strangers, and the patience to allow such reciprocity to have its own rewards demonstrate attitudes most conducive to culture learning and cross-cultural adaptation.

Reciprocity has its problems, of course. What your host culture would like to give you may not be what you really want. You hope your colleague at the office in Tokyo invites you to go skiing with him during Christmas vacation; instead his Christmas gift to you is a Japanese print. You intend your house call to the Greek acquaintance to be merely a brief inquiry about the youth hostels; he insists on your staying the entire day, a day that you had hoped to spend alone with your American friends. You contract with a guide to take your group to see the waterfalls; he takes you, instead, to a town festival that features a parade because he thinks the festivities to be more important than the waterfalls.

Further, what your host culture would like for you to give them may not be what you are ready to give. The Filipino family that hosted you so generously now seems to expect your continued association with them, even your support (and hosting) of their children. The president of the club who eagerly agreed to talk with your group about the changing role of women in the country has now asked you to make a personal contact with the American consul on her behalf. She wants a two-year visa to the United States.

Effective reciprocity begins in events that may seem trivial, but which represent effective cross-cultural communications. Reciprocity may become institutional or national in scope. A town that hosts American students requests and is reimbursed not with money but with an ambulance that is made in the students' college town. The two cities become sisters. The countries eventually modify their systems of tariffs to effect fairer trading with each other.

In summary, the traveler with a positive attitude toward cross-cultural reciprocity thinks of a trip, from beginning to end, not in terms of personal gain but rather in terms of opportunities for sharing. That kind of attitude helps cultures bridge their differences.

Character traits

What kind of personality does a successful culture learner have? Are there differences in the character traits of the person who is not only willing but eager to become a culture learner and the person who retreats from the challenge?

International program directors wish they had some answers to this question. A widely known and respected international service program was recently asked by its field representative for sixteen volunteers. The home office came up with them, but one dropped out at the airport just before departure from the United States. When the team arrived in the country, two volunteers turned around and went home. A couple of days later during the first orientation sessions, two more left. Two more were asked to leave before they had even settled in to their assignments. Nine of the sixteen remained for the work. "What a waste of time and energy!" the field representative said. "The home office ought to improve its screening."

Indeed, it should. For a number of years I have assisted in the orientation program of another international agency, smaller than the one referred to above. Typically this latter agency has about a thousand people in the field, many of them overseas. To characterize those assignments, I turn to words such as demanding, dangerous, undefined, complex, exhausting, and significant. Yet the rate of early returnees is extremely low.

Why would Agency A lose seven of sixteen volunteers in one assignment and Agency B lose so few?

The answer is not obvious. Administrative competence of the organizations is not the critical factor. Both agencies are run well. Education level is not the answer. Agency A volunteers have a higher average education than Agency B, many with master's degrees. Economic levels, skill levels, language facility, length of orientation—none of these factors satisfactorily explains the adaptability and success of one group of volunteers in contrast to the other. The answer lies instead in the fact that Agency B looked for certain character traits in the people it selected, traits that predisposed them to success in cross-cultural situations. Agency A did not.

Character traits which influence intercultural competence

What are these traits? While researchers have explored the predictability of intercultural success, the data continue to be tentative, somewhat contradictory, and quite general. We, therefore, don't know if there is an ideal intercultural personality, but we have some clues. I also have my own experience of working with overseas educational and service programs for many years. What I've tried to do here is describe the kinds of persons I have found to be most successful in our programs, and have come up with ten preferred traits (expressed as comparatives).

1. A curious rather than a passive person. I'm referring to the group member who, on a trip to the hot and noisy sugar mill, pushes nearer to the guide to shout questions about the factory process, about sugar cultivation, and about the industry, while others follow on behind.

2. A trusting rather than a suspicious person. In a journey to another culture, an individual entrusts himself or herself to others. There's no other way to get through the journey.

3. A brave rather than a fearful person. On occasion I have had difficulty distinguishing bravery from daring and even foolhardiness among the rascals I have worked with, and yet this kind of valiant explorer soon climbs higher than the cautious ones.

4. A secure rather than a guarded person. The individual who has a strong self-concept will likely be confident in new situations. Insecure individuals feel threatened rather easily.

5. A laid-back, relaxed person rather than an impatient one. This has to do with time—some people can bend easily to accommodate the pace of the local environment. Others can't.

6. A teachable rather than a finished person. It's easy to detect the difference. One person has already closed the book. The other is ready for new experiences and new understandings, motivated to change and grow.

7. A friendly rather than a diligent person. The latter has a list of things to accomplish while the former gives first place to people.

8. A humble rather than a haughty person. Arrogance produces "the ugly American." Humility corresponds with genuineness.

9. A compassionate or empathetic person rather than an insensitive one. I'm not talking here about the do-gooder, but rather the person with the capacity and the will to identify with the circumstances of others.

10. A person with a sense of humor rather than a humorless one. Yes, laughter is the best medicine overseas also.

Even while this informal list was being tested over the years by firsthand experience, it grew as I read the work of practitioners and scholars who have tried to define intercultural competence. L. Robert Kohls in his widely used *Survival Kit for Overseas Living* (1996) identifies sixteen traits that contribute to cultural adjustment, most of which overlap with my list. Several deserve special mention here.

1. Low goal/task orientation. Kohls says that a person who is less compelled and preoccupied by a work

assignment is likely to be more open to social inter-actions and consequently quicker to adapt to cultural challenges.

2. Nonjudgmentalness. This has to do with a person's ability to "roll with the punches" without making early and prejudicial evaluations of people and situations. This person has a high tolerance level for differences encountered.

3. Flexibility, adaptability. The ability to make basic changes in thought patterns, experience new ways of feeling, and adopt behavioral changes. The contrast-ing trait is rigidity.

4. Communicativeness. How could I have failed to put this item on my first list? It has to do, of course, with verbal and nonverbal aptitudes—listening, observing, and responding. One's ability to be perceptive relates to one's capacity to be insightful.

5. Warmth in human relationships. Kohls is referring to something beyond communication skills. By using the term "warmth" he is directing attention to a particu-lar kind of personality affect that encourages com-fortable interaction.

6. Motivation. It's rather obvious that a person who truly wants to be a sojourner will be a better culture learner than one who is forced into the situation.

7. Self-reliance. The person of positive self-concept, in-tegrity, and courage will adapt most easily to the chal-lenge of culture learning.

8. Ability to fail. Kohls considers this trait to be one of the most important. The person who is tolerant of his or her own mistakes and tries to learn from them, rather than bemoan imperfections, has more poten-tial for rapid and effective adaptation in new situa-tions.

Finally, I'd like to call particular attention to several char-acter traits that seem to commend themselves powerfully. They are a person's (1) breadth of affiliation, (2) tolerance for ambiguity, (3) general receptivity, and (4) capacity for empa-thy.

Breadth of affiliation

The kinds of affiliations a person has may be seen as a trait contributing to intercultural competence. It has to do with belonging and pertains to the groups one becomes a part of, the social configuration that gives a person a social identity. One is affiliated with family, school, church, region, and possibly an ethnic community. Occasionally in class I ask students to record all their affiliations. These lists eventually include 50, 75, and even 100 items.

The nature of one's affiliations contributes significantly to one's readiness (or lack thereof) to meet strangers, inasmuch as the group's disposition to outsiders impresses itself upon each individual (Stewart and Bennett 1991). Each cultural group holds a set of attitudes about distant and dissimilar cultures; affiliated group members are likely to hold the same attitudes.

Xenophobic groups—those fearful or contemptuous of strangers or foreigners—provide a scaffolding to support their ethnocentric disposition. They foster prejudices, build fences, and discourage their members from venturing into strangers' lands. In contrast, culturally tolerant groups urge their members to meet strangers and to extend themselves when doing so.

The success rate for Agency B described earlier in this chapter (see p. 15) has a great deal to do with affiliation. Its constituency is positively motivated for cross-cultural contacts. It is not unusual for those constituents to travel, live, and work overseas. There is even an expectation in churches, homes, and communities of that constituency—even among its youth—of spending one, two, or three years in an overseas service assignment.

In sharp contrast is the agency that has to deal with a constituency not positively motivated for cross-cultural contacts, where families have rarely ventured out of their own communities, where people are not hospitable to strangers of other ethnic origins or races, and where learning foreign languages and studying other cultures are considered boring subjects in school.

Tolerance for ambiguity

Ambiguity is another element in the intercultural experience to which scholars have given attention (Brislin 1981; Dodd

1987; Grove and Torbiörn 1993; Gudykunst and Kim 1984b; Ruben 1977). It too is presented as a function of multiculturalism and is expressed something like this: one measure of a person's potential for multiculturalism may be indicated in his or her capacity to tolerate or accommodate ambiguity.

Consider its opposite. A person with little tolerance for ambiguity insists upon clear definitions, precision, predictability, satisfied expectations, and, above all, knowing with certainty what is happening or is about to happen. Such a person needs to know prior to the field trip whether there will be warm showers, when breakfast will be served, whether the water will be safe to drink, and when the group will return.

Here's a specific case. Marjorie, a student abroad, happily invited her host family to a roller-skating party sponsored by her college. Because of her limited facility in using the local language and because roller-skating was not yet a well-known recreation (only a couple of rinks in the country), she gave her host parents a printed invitation and explanation. She concluded by their expressions that they accepted the invitation and shared her enthusiasm. Sunday, the day of the skating party, arrived. To Marjorie's surprise, the parents announced in the morning that the family was going to the country for a picnic. But what about the skating party, Marjorie tried to ask. They assured Marjorie that they'd return in the afternoon for roller-skating. Thereupon they—along with Marjorie—left for the outing. In the afternoon, they said they'd soon be returning to the city, but they didn't. An hour later they repeated their intention of packing up, but they didn't. They finally began their return to the city when the roller-skating party was over.

Why did the family indicate they would go to the party and then pursue other plans? Was it intentional? Was there a religious scruple against the event? Perhaps the father, who was somewhat authoritarian, didn't want to go, and so ruled the family according to his wishes? Maybe the family was socially ill at ease with other host families? Did they think it would cost them money? Were they timid about trying to skate?

The situation—while it was in progress—tested Marjorie to the extreme. Would she, or would she not, accommodate this ambiguity? On the one hand, she could allow herself to be upset by the confusion and express her disappointment and frustration with their inconsistent behavior. On the other, she could acknowledge to herself the continuing presence of mysteries in this foreign land, accommodate the strange and incongruous behavior, and make the most of a family outing, hoping that someday she would better understand.

General receptivity

To illustrate the idea of receptivity, I use the metaphor of gatekeeping. The keeper of the gate has the responsibility of letting something in, or of shutting something out. By nature and training, most of us are expert gatekeepers, and we keep most of what happens around us out. For example, we are exposed to a multitude of advertisements and commercial messages daily. Some studies say the number adds up to more than 1500 for an urban dweller. With so many messages hitting us, we'd go crazy by 10:00 A.M. if we weren't expert at screening the messages out. Our attention is selective in what we consciously hear, see, feel, and taste (indeed, technically it is called "selective perception").

So it is with social and cultural issues. Located inside a cultural group, we keep the gates. As I read the daily paper, for instance, this kind of gatekeeping is going on constantly. I pause to read what has happened in my town, but skim the events of a neighboring village. I am more receptive to news of my country than news of others.

This natural tendency has important consequences. As we screen things out, we circumscribe the kinds of information that will affect us. Those limited pieces of information shape our view of the world. So we exercise our gatekeeping skills, trying to make wise decisions of what to keep out and what to let in.

To become multicultural, there must be a measure of receptivity not only in allowing new information through the gates, but also in revising our view of things once we absorb it. An ethnocentric person lives according to the gag line: "My mind is made up, don't confuse me with the facts." A multicultural person, on the other hand, is always ready to modify a sense of the world and of him- or herself on the basis of new evidence. This readiness is more than a superficial tolerance of things strange. Rather it implies a willingness to change a frame of reference so as to see things from another's point of view.

Capacity for empathy

Another key component of the multicultural personality is the ability to empathize (Bennett 1979; Broome 1991; Casse 1981; Luce and Smith 1987; Stewart and Bennett 1991). Empathy is related to, but distinct from, sympathy. If you have sympathy, you express pity or sorrow for the distress of another person. The sympathy, however, is determined by how you would feel if you were in that person's place. It is oriented to one's self. Since, you might say, I typically feel this way about such things, my friend probably feels this way too.

If you have empathy, on the other hand, you can identify with the feelings of the other person on that person's terms. "Empathy relies on the ability to temporarily set aside one's own perception of the world and assume an alternative perspective," say Stewart and Bennett. "Self-interest and purposes are held in check as one attempts to place oneself in the immediate situation and field (but not in the shoes) of another" (1991, 152).

An empathetic person picks up seemingly disconnected cues and makes coherent sense out of them. Many of these cues arise not so much from the words or explicit gestures of the other person, as from the social and cultural context in which the other person lives. As scholars try to articulate this concept of empathy, I recall the empathetic participants in our programs overseas—those who were less concerned about their own first-day nervousness than about the insecurities of the host family as its members welcomed a stranger into their homes. On field trips they were the ones to empathize with the tour guide whose voice quivered because she had never explained the factory before to a group of visitors. Empathetic volunteers seemed to learn quickly which child at the orphanage needed to be held and hugged.

The multicultural personality

This chapter has emphasized the importance of attitudes and character traits in the culture learner. Even in the absence of a definitive model of the culturally competent person, the attitudes and traits do comprise a tentative picture that at least can be contrasted with the attitudes and traits that discourage culture learning. For example, see chapter 1 on the way a person can be "located" on the culture-learning continuum.

As you will recall from that explanation, the culture-learning continuum is marked at one extreme by ethnocentrism and at the other by multiculturalism (or ethnorelativism). At the ethnocentrism extreme is the person fully immersed in his or her own culture with no sense that there are other valid sets of perceptions, structures of thought, or attitudes and behaviors. To this person the possibility of connections with a world beyond one's own culture is ruled out. An ethnocentric personality is defined and fenced in by the norms of one particular ethnicity.

In contrast, the person at the multiculturalism end of the continuum is culturally mobile. His or her own sense of self is molded continually by new cultural contacts and new relationships. (See Bennett 1993; Bochner 1981; Gudykunst and Kim 1984a; Kim and Gudykunst 1988; Sarbaugh 1988; Triandis 1990.)

Young Yun Kim, who has researched and written extensively on intercultural issues, has explored what she calls the "intercultural person."

> The intercultural person represents a type of person whose cognitive, affective, and behavioral characteristics are not limited but are open to growth beyond the psychological parameters of his or her own culture.... With an openness toward change, a willingness to revise our own cultural premises, and the enthusiasm to work it through, we are on the way to cultivating our fullest human potentialities and to contributing our share in this enormous process of civilizational change (1991, 401-11).

The notion of a culture-learning continuum can be especially helpful for the person inclined to be categorical. It is not a question of whether one is or is not qualified to be a culture learner. It is more helpful to think of every potential culture learner as located at some point on the continuum, but not forever fixed at that position. Rather, each is capable of growing, of moving on the continuum toward ethnorelativism.

Chapter 3

Methods in Culture Learning: The Action-Reflection-Response Strategy

In the previous chapter, we discussed the *attitudes* and *traits* which contribute to successful culture learning. In this chapter and the following one we turn our attention to the *skills* needed for productive culture learning.

This chapter is devoted to one particular model well suited to culture learning, the action-reflection-response strategy, which is perhaps more commonly known as experiential learning.

To define the action-reflection-response strategy, let's contrast it with another one, the theory-application model.

This latter model uses a two-part sequence: first, you learn a theory; second, you put that theory into practice. The theory-application model pervades Western colleges and universities, learned societies, science, industry, and theology. While the applications of this model vary widely, students using it are expected to listen, to absorb, and sometimes to memorize, for they later will have occasion to apply what they have learned. The following assumptions support this model: (1) learning is a rational process, dominated by rigorous thought; (2) learning is linear—things happen in sequence; (3) the best learning is efficient, with wasteful and costly trial and error eliminated; (4) learning is hierarchical, in that the specialist with knowledge becomes the teacher of those without knowledge.

In rather sharp contrast, action-reflection-response learning features three elements in a sequence quite different from the previous model:

Action. You may call it praxis, practicum, field experience, learning on the job, doing it, or any other appropriate term.

Reflection. This is the process of attaining greater knowledge of something as a result of thinking through the action, a process made possible through gaining more information about, assimilating, and accepting ownership of the experience.

Response. The new knowing isn't enough; there must be a corresponding attitudinal or behavioral modification.

Action-reflection-response learning in intercultural settings

We frequently ask people in highly structured overseas educational programs why they, who have invested so dearly and traveled so far to learn about a foreign culture, now sit in classrooms and read textbooks. Clearly, one can obtain valuable information about one's host country from books and lectures. They are also useful at certain stages of the language-learning process. But for culture learning there is no substitute for direct encounter.

The intercultural setting is both the classroom and the text for culture learning. In every contact a visitor has within a new environment there is potential for learning.

Even fairly routine experiences are material for the action-reflection-response learning process. Some experiences of students in overseas study and service-learning programs suggest where these opportunities lie.

Sojourners who are not students will need to identify other examples more relevant to them.

What follows is an illustration of the action-reflection-response strategy involving a kind of instant replay of important and/or memorable experiences. It is called "reviewing critical events."

Reviewing critical events

In televised athletics, the instant replay contributes to more accurate sports analysis. Prior to replays, the fan experienced a play so briefly that the memory of the particulars was sometimes closer to fantasy than fact. Cameras can now show a reenactment from several angles and in slow motion. Thanks to instant replay, a critical event in sports can be made both more understandable and more enjoyable.

In intercultural encounters, too, there are critical events, the understanding and management, if not enjoyment, of which can be improved by a kind of instant replay we call "reviewing critical events." Some of these events are exciting, many are memorable. Occasionally they are baffling, some are hurtful. Almost all have their moments of frustration. Unfortunately (or perhaps fortunately!) there are no cameras involved in these reviews of critical events. But there are ways to give our intercultural encounters a second run-through that allows us to experience them in slow motion, so to speak, and to be able to analyze them in greater detail and understand them better.

Most travelers abroad don't have to be coaxed to tell stories of their encounters with the strange and foreign, ranging from asking incorrectly for food in a restaurant to accidentally insulting an important official. What is less usual, however, is a systematic study of these misadventures. It is here that our instant replay comes in. Reviewing critical events includes the following steps:

1. recognizing what a critical event is,
2. reconstructing the event,

3. getting more information about it, and

4. making new interpretations and shaping new behavior as a result of it.

Let's go through a critical event step by step, identifying how each step is crucial to the end result.

Step 1

Recognizing the critical event. It is understandable that a stranger in a foreign land can sometimes be under such stress as to be unable to isolate any one critical event out of the grand confusion. Most can, however, delineate particular moments of frustration which can be called back for replay.

> One morning in downtown San José, I became conscious of how angry I felt. I realized that I was angry because my day had gotten off to a bad start when I was pulled over by a traffic cop, who scolded me for kindly stopping my car to let two old men walk across the street.

The act of being stopped by the officer and my subsequent anger was a critical event.

Step 2

Reconstructing the critical event. In a critical event there is a setting in which people are acting or interacting in a more or less routine way. Something happens which breaks the routine, something unexpected that intensifies or modifies the action and draws out different behaviors. A drama of some sort unfolds. Eventually there is a climax to the action, for good or bad, and then a denouement in which there may be apologies, congratulations, efforts to pick up some of the pieces—or it may be an event in which the denouement occurs entirely within the individual as he or she mulls over what happened.

> You see, I jumped into my Toyota, having fourteen chores neatly listed on an index card in my shirt pocket. I headed for town and as I came past Calderón Guardia Hospital, I noticed two men—certainly older than seventy—with hospital gowns on, standing by the curb, wanting to cross from the hospital to the row of

doctors' offices on the other side of the street. But Latin drivers, being the way they are, rudely drove through, prohibiting the two feeble men from crossing. Generously, and might one say gallantly, I stopped the car right in the middle of the two lanes, so that no careless, insistent driver of a delivery truck or bus could get around and hit the men. I motioned them; they hobbled across, to the accompaniment of many horns. Once they were on the other side, I resumed... only to be whistled to the curb by a traffic cop who scolded me for what I did. So there we had a Latin American policeman, probably a corrupt, bribe-taking cop, supporting the chaotic and dangerous habits of Latin American drivers. Naturally, I was furious.

I retell the event as I experienced it, including all of the facts and feelings that I can remember.

Step 3

Getting more information. Once you have reconstructed the event as well as you can, it's time to get more information. This new data can come from a variety of sources. In the first place, your telling the story to another person may elicit comments or possibly some questions the asking of which forces you to recall additional data. More typically, you involve an informant, someone qualified by experience in or knowledge of the culture, to provide more information about the nature of and background to the event. Invariably this informant helps you see things you had not seen before.

This is dumb, I said to myself. Here I am in San José, burning up in fury and thus not able to get my fourteen chores done. Why not deal with the critical event of the morning? So I retrieved my car from the parking garage (it had been there a total of five minutes) and drove back to the hospital, parking near the cop. I walked over to him, and introduced myself—"the person you pulled over"—and when he looked stunned I pointed out my car.

31

Oh, yes, he recognized me, but gazed at me without expression. Why, I asked him, did he pull me over? I, a foreigner, was puzzled by his action. I thought I was doing a kindness. Now I returned, because I wanted to learn, so as not to repeat the offense. His face relaxed, he touched me on the arm. "Mister...you see, this is a hospital... and those are doctors' offices...and this hospital complex is located here in Barrio Aranjuez...its streets, you can notice, are very narrow... we have traffic problems, many impossible traffic jams.... But Mister, there is only one street leading into the Barrio, and on that street come the ambulances from Cartago, from Tres Rios, from Guadalupe, Moravia, and Coronado. If the traffic is stalled, the ambulances can't get through. So I am stationed here to keep traffic moving. As for patients needing to go to the doctors' offices, they are clearly instructed to come to this corner, and I help them across. Mister, can you understand?"

What good luck I had. One of the very persons involved in my critical event was still available to serve as informant. Problem was, I had to show my embarrassment right in front of him.

Step 4

Making new interpretations of the event. When you have accumulated information, preferably from several different points of view (it won't always be as easy as it was for me), the facts illuminate each other and bring to light new aspects of the event. At this point, if you can face the fact that your ability to perceive reality, especially in cross-cultural situations, is limited, you can begin to make new interpretations and possibly some behavioral adjustments.

I was dumbstruck, by both his manner and his facts. He was not the scolding traffic officer, but a personable Costa Rican, filled with goodwill and no small amount of charm. I thanked him, and as I walked away, I began to recall the judgments I had earlier made: Latin drivers, my own superiority, police stupidity and corruption. As I thought of my set of interpretations, I recognized how completely I was absorbed in my own cultural cocoon, my own day's agenda, and my own righteousness. The anger that I had earlier felt now changed into an altogether different feeling—embarrassment and chagrin, although as I drove downtown again, I was rather pleased that I had the courage to go talk with the police officer and further my own culture learning.

Examining critical events, even with reconstruction and additional data and reinterpretation, won't always ease the stress of intercultural misadventures. Nor will critical events always reveal their complexities to you, as did the incident above. Some critical events, no matter how hard one works to understand them, can leave you angry, diminished, and even permanently scarred. But they are the exception. The majority of critical events beg to be used for learning about and coming to understand and enjoy the strangers you meet in your intercultural experience.

Action	Reflection	Response
routines surrounding the use of the bathroom in a new family household	reviewing and analyzing by oneself critical events and personal encounters with host nationals and/or the host culture	discussed earlier
planning and departing on field trips		integrating more effectively into one's host family
undertaking independent study projects on aspects of the local community or the host culture, such as how farming is done	gathering additional information about the context in which these events and encounters occurred	building relationships with local people
interviewing host nationals about local issues	reading about intercultural and other relevant issues	changing attitudes, opinions, values, and philosophies
		reshaping one's understanding of U.S. foreign policy
		rewriting personal financial budgets

Action	Reflection	Response
working with a local agency providing social services to disabled veterans	keeping a regular journal	revising career plans
	discussing individual experiences in daily or weekly group meetings or seminars	modifying choice of college major
	giving follow-up reports to the group on subjects	

Summary

Methods of learning vary widely. What we may suppose is the best or universal way to teach children is likely to be a way shaped largely by a teacher's creativity and the force of the child's culture. In the West, we have relied on versions of a theory-application sequence to learning. We adhere to that sequence in a variety of ways, including the use of lecture followed by discussion.

Intercultural settings provide appropriate occasions to engage in another kind of educational approach—action-reflection-response learning. Anyone in an intercultural setting can use this model for culture learning and personal growth. The critical events which happen universally to travelers and sojourners abroad are the supplied action. All the individual has to do is add the systematic analysis of it.

The approach favored in this book is based on and encourages the use of the action-reflection-response strategy. While here we have focused on the reviewing of critical events, later exercises will introduce yet other approaches to and styles of this strategy.

Chapter 4

Methods in Culture Learning: Reflection as Cultural Analysis

Learning a second language as an adult is a different process from learning one's first language as a child. The first one comes naturally because, according to Noam Chomsky, at birth one is programmed to learn any language (1972). As a person grows older, the original state of language preparedness is changed and limited. Language learning gradually becomes a more difficult task, shifting from a natural to an artificial process.

So it is with culture learning. A child learns the first culture naturally and unconsciously. An adult learns a second culture only with considerable effort. If the learning is to be truly effective, it must entail, as mentioned earlier, not only cognitive, but also affective and behavioral changes.

Milton J. Bennett reminds us that successful culture learning is more than acquisition of new skills (1986, 179). A mastery of culture demands new awareness and attitudes. The same sentiments are expressed by David Hoopes:

> The critical element in the expansion of intercultural learning is not the fullness with which one knows each culture, but the degree to which the processes of cross-cultural learning, communication and human relations have been mastered (1979, 20).

Particularly challenging for the culture learner is the mental and emotional processing indicated by the term *reflection* in the action-reflection-response strategy. How does one effectively grasp the meaning of a critical event and the essence of a new culture, understanding it in sufficient depth not only to appreciate its dynamic complexities but also to function comfortably as a participant?

The term reflection labels a collection of activities we commonly refer to as analysis. But the word "analysis" may, because of our preconceptions about what it is, hide as much as it reveals of the full range of activities we are calling reflection: searching, finding, seeing, identifying, naming, categorizing, classifying, interpreting—these are only a small part of reflection.

What, then, is the best way to reflect upon—or analyze—intercultural experience so that it ultimately yields a holistic pattern of culture learning? In this chapter, we examine a few samples of cultural analyses produced by scholars in the field. This brief walk-through is not intended to be a comprehensive review of the literature on the subject, but rather a citing of models that a beginning culture learner might try to imitate in a fashion appropriate for making on-site inquiries. Some of the guides build upon these examples.

Field observation

Margaret Mead, one of the twentieth century's leading anthropologists, followed in the footsteps of Ruth Benedict to clear a path in the use of field observation in anthropological research. Mead's accomplishments will endure even though later scholars improved on the validity, reliability, and objectivity of her methods.

Mead proposed to learn about the life of adolescent girls in selected so-called primitive sites in the Southwest Pacific by going there, observing, making careful notes, trying to find recurring behaviors, identifying patterns in those behaviors, and finally making some generalizations that fit what she saw (1963).

In another significant study, Mead observed three cultures—the Arapesh of New Guinea, the Manus of the southern coast of the Admiralty Islands, and the people of Bali. Her goal was to investigate the relationship of geography, subsistence, and communication in each setting and subsequently to determine how each respective community organized its social controls (1948).

What can today's culture learner gain from Mead's early work? The value of disciplined observation. The kind of research Mead did—and the kind we are recommending in the action-reflection-response strategy—demands, in the first place, a careful defining of what one is looking at or looking for. To focus on selected aspects of a culture or particular relationships is likely to yield more than a vague, undifferentiated attempt to be aware of culture. Second, it requires apprehending with all of the senses what a culture reveals about itself. Third—and Mead raised this to both a science and an art—it calls for making minute observations on which to build a generalized description of the culture. One must always do this task tentatively, ready to admit new and contradictory information. It can take a long time and a great deal of careful observation to gather the information which makes the data add up to a coherent description. Some of the guides are designed collaterally, if not primarily, to help you become a better observer. See especially Guides 3, 11, and 12.

Factor analysis

Edward T. Hall has produced a series of classic books about the dimensions of culture in which the most important similarities and differences lie. Reference was made earlier to his work on the relationship of cultural context and meaning; here we refer to an earlier product of his fertile mind. Like

Mead, Hall is a culture observer. And like Mead, he knows the importance of focusing his attention on particular aspects— let's call them factors—of culture. His work, then, has became a form of factor analysis, a term used here in a nonstatistical sense.

For example, Hall identified communication as a cultural activity. He knew, of course, that people of all cultures send messages back and forth, so he set himself the task of finding out what was common across cultures in message sending. He concluded that all cultures, while their messages might be different, used similar primary message systems. He then developed a kind of factor analysis of primary message systems:

1. Interaction—messages having to do with verbal and nonverbal exchanges between people as they maintain contact with each other, such as greetings or conversations.

2. Association—messages having to do with grouping and affiliations.

3. Subsistence—messages having to do with making a living, one's job, chores, eating, etc.

4. Sexuality—messages having to do with dating and mating, procreation, and survival.

5. Territoriality—messages having to do with the structure and use of space.

6. Temporality—messages having to do with the definitions, functions, and use of time.

7. Learning—messages having to do with acculturation, assimilation, and the passing on of a heritage.

8. Play—messages having to do with diversionary activity, laughter, games, etc.

9. Defense—messages having to do with self- and communal protection, war, fighting, etc.

10. Exploitation—messages having to do with the handling of tools, the manipulation of material properties (1973, 57-81).

Hall's model has in subsequent years been reformulated by other scholars, but the notion that there can be ways to factor out any one aspect of a culture becomes a valuable tool for the culture learner. Each factor can then become a new field for further inquiry, as Hall himself has demonstrated in his book-length studies of the use of time, *The Dance of Life: The Other Dimension of Time* (1983) and space, *The Hidden Dimension* (1966).

Beginning culture learners might try to make a factor analysis of some kind, perhaps of words and gestures that people use to express "How are you?" and "I'm fine, thank you." Or they might explore the kinds of structures that families live in—single-family houses, row houses, apartments, etc. Or they can examine the major means of conveyances people use to get from home to work each day. As you can see, factor analysis can help you ferret out information that a casual observer would miss. (See Guides 6 and 11 for projects related to an analysis of factors.)

Ethnography

The term ethnography may be broadly defined as the description of cultures, or, in somewhat more restricted terms, as a particular way to go about the task. I am using the term in the latter sense. Ethnography is the study and description of culture from inside it, or from the culture's own point of view. In contrast is the study of culture from the outside, using outside models and methods, perspectives, categories, definitions, and interpretations.

The culture learner can get a good introduction to ethnographic studies from the writings of James P. Spradley and David W. McCurdy (1972). These are the procedures: you define a cultural scene for your study; you go inside it to find cultural informants; you observe what is happening; and you ask questions that will elicit from the informant a response which reflects that particular culture's ways of perceiving, its internal logic, its social system, its value patterns, and so forth. You use what Spradley and McCurdy call *structural* questions to allow the informant to define the culture in its own terms. From the culture itself, then, you elicit the cultural meanings.

Spradley and McCurdy have studied many cultures, subcultures, and cultural scenes in this way, including those of tramps, hitchhikers, and high school girls. Using the information gained from inside the culture group itself, they attempt to build taxonomies that show how the people of the culture define and categorize themselves. Here is a hypothetical case of a taxonomic definition of a kindergarten, as seen and expressed by a kindergarten pupil whom we shall name Tina.

A taxonomy of kindergarten as Tina sees it

people	pulls hair and hits	cries	snacks with me	sits at my table
Randy	yes	no	no	yes
Peter	no	yes	no	no
Anna	no	no	yes	yes
Kimberly	no	yes	yes	no

This taxonomy is used to illustrate that the insider's structures and categories are likely to be different from the outsider's. One might imagine the outsider wanting to impose categories of socioeconomic status, sex, intelligence, verbal skills, age, and family structure. Further, the taxonomy suggests to the ethnographer what kindergarten means to Tina and her classmates. Hitting, pulling hair, and crying might be principal shapers of meaning for the children themselves.

An example of a widely read and appreciated ethnographic study of this kind is Thomas Kochman's *Black and White Styles in Conflict* (1981). Kochman shows the close relationship between language and behavior in the African-American community by entering into the culture and allowing its own meanings to inform his interpretations. An outsider, using outside white definitions of "colored people," would not have been able to grasp what Kochman did.

Analysis of cues, symbols, and signs

Cultures reveal themselves by way of "words and things." Every culture has its conventions, verbal and nonverbal, for conveying meaning. Let's look at one particular cultural scene from this perspective.

Recently, as I entered the classroom on the first day of the trimester, I became aware—with hardly a visual sweep of the room—that the students were not seated in a random and meaningless disorder. As usual, there was the large clustering in the middle, more or less in front of me. Then there were some others: one lone person in the front row, almost against the instructor's table; three people in the back row behind the others; a student off to the right; and a student off to the left and against the wall, with vacant chairs between him and the others. Of the students on the fringes, I was most aware of the chap on the left. His body was turned a bit toward the wall. His gaze was directed straight ahead or toward the wall. He maintained no contact with classmates. He was an African American.

Only later did I learn that the student off to the right had come back to college after being out for a period of time and had recently been to a rehab center. Of the three in the rear, one dropped out after the first class period, the second was Catholic (the campus was predominantly Protestant) and a commuter who, because of not living in the dorm, had few friends on campus, and the third, I soon found out, wrote essays about depression. The student up front was hard of hearing.

The students in the center of the class were, one might say, in the center of this cultural scene. Those at the edges were in some manner marginal. While the details of my students' integration into and estrangement from the campus scene were not clear to me when I first entered the classroom, I did nonetheless feel that something meaningful was being presented to me, that there was some kind of nonverbal message here.

The first essay from Greg, the African-American student, was filled with pain and violence but did not reveal much of himself. He read it in class. As he became more comfortable, he wrote more candidly. In one composition, he told of walking out of a local grocery store and seeing a van-load of young women quickly roll up the windows and lock the doors in fear as he approached his car which was parked next to theirs. On another occasion he gave a presentation on black hairstyles and talked of their significance. He abandoned the chair by the wall and mixed with the main body of students. The other students who had seated themselves marginally to the rest of the class at first also changed their seating during the course of the semester, moving sometimes closer, sometimes farther away.

At the end of the term, I learned that a student who sat from the beginning in the middle with the in-group was quite disappointed in the class and expressed criticism that bordered on hostility. The root of the problem: none of her essays was ever read publicly or duplicated or shown on the overhead projector for class discussion. It was coincidental; none of her writing had seemed appropriate for discussion by the full class. But she took it as a signal; she felt there was a message in the exclusion of her essays—just as I had felt there was a message in the way the students seated themselves on the first day.

In that classroom there were many more exchanges of meaning, conveyed verbally and nonverbally. Sometimes I caught the signs, sometimes I didn't. As a teacher I have been trying to pay better attention to all of the signals—the chair that a student selects, where their eyes focus and their intensity, the clothing and how it is worn, the handwriting in their essays, the kind of interaction with classmates, the form of entering and leaving the room—because the number and kind of elements that make up a communication act are far more diverse than I had ever imagined. And if I understand more of the messages that are being given off in a classroom—and understand them better—I think I can be a more effective teacher.

Cultures are similar to that college classroom. Every culture has its way of signing (commonly referred to as nonverbal communication). To the insiders, the sign system is natural, largely unconscious—almost like breathing. Meanings are given to subtle cues. A word takes on special connotations. A gesture comes into use and gradually changes its meaning and then is discarded. To an outsider, this sign system will likely seem impenetrable because the outsider has had no part in making those meanings in the first place. Guides 2 and 6 address the topic of sign analysis.

Myth analysis

Joseph Campbell was one of a number of scholars who have used myth analysis to understand cultures. (An example of his many works is *The Power of Myth* 1988.) The list ranges from Edith Hamilton who studied Greek myths (*The Greek Way* 1971) to Leszek Kolakowski, a professor from Poland who has written about modern cultures in *The Presence of Myth* (1989). The list includes widely recognized names such as Roland Barthes, Bruno Bettelheim, Mircea Eliade, Jacques Ellul, Northrup Frye, Carl Jung, and many others.

Myth analysis tries, through the study of a people's myths, to understand their way of life, what they know and believe, how they relate to nature, what they do with inexplicable happenings, how they adjust to change, and how they understand basic human phenomena such as birth and death. Myth analysts study the "wisdom" that flows from generation to generation, often couched in story, anecdote, fairy tale, legend, and sayings.

Campbell, for example, has studied the hero (1990) and the goddess (1991) as mythic figures. These studies help the scholar to understand what a culture values in its men and women and how it defines roles, develops its expectations, and articulates its rules and sanctions.

While the culture learner is likely not to be an accomplished myth analyst, this field of activity suggests to even the beginner that using current clues (wall hangings, superstitions, statues downtown, a TV serial, the explanation for an earthquake) offers a way to discover some of the myths upon which the culture is founded (see Guides 1, 5, and 9).

As a final note, it is helpful to recognize that learning by analysis is the Western way to learn, as Camille Paglia reminds us in *Sexual Personae* (1990).

> Science is a method of logical analysis of nature's [culture's] operations.... Western science is a product of the Apollonian mind: its hope is that by naming and classification, by the cold light of intellect, archaic night can be pushed back and defeated.
>
> Name and person are part of the West's quest for form. The West insists on the discrete identity of objects. To name is to know; to know is to control.... Far Eastern culture has never striven against nature in this way. Compliance, not confrontation is its rule. Buddhist meditation seeks the unity and harmony of reality (5).

One might suggest that the West learns by taking things apart, the East by putting things together. Culture learning, however, takes things apart *and* puts things together. The methods of analysis described here, combined with the action-reflection-response strategy, do not end with things in pieces and with the person paralyzed. Rather, they lead into an attitudinal and behavioral response that we hope may be characterized by the word *growth*.

Chapter 5

Culture Learning, Values, and Ethical Choices

Culture learning at its best is inclusive, not only in the scope of one's involvement (cognitive, affective and behavioral), but also in the range of life that is brought into the curriculum. Culture learning includes everything—a people's history, industry, art, institutions, communication patterns, and values. It is the issue of values that calls for further discussion in this chapter.

A study of cultural values suggests three major questions:

1. Must you forsake the values of your culture and people when you aspire to be a multicultural person?

2. Are you entitled to judge the host culture's value system?

3. Does cultural relativity lead to a deterioration of values or, indeed, to moral chaos?

To begin these explorations, please rank the eight behaviors below in the order of their moral rightness.

- a woman slipping $20 to a traffic officer who intends to give her a citation
- a man urinating by the road
- a woman talking to another driver from out of the car window at a traffic light
- a woman throwing a dishpan of water out of the window and onto the street
- a man arguing vehemently on the verge of violence, raising his fists at the driver of another vehicle that had hit him
- a woman kicking a cow off the path so that she can continue on her way
- a man setting up a rock barrier so that people cannot continue using the street
- a woman spreading out a sheet on the sidewalk, on which she intends to show items for sale

If you are an American from Iowa you are likely to have considered most of the items to be a little odd, although you'd see nothing wrong in talking to another driver from out of your own car window, and surely you'd chase off the cow without pangs of conscience. On the other side, you'd say that some of the items are unacceptable, such as setting up a rock barricade or paying off the cop. Urinating in a public place can lead to an arrest. It would be crude to throw kitchen water out the window. And in downtown Keokuk, they don't even allow bicycles on the sidewalk, much less a huckster.

But if you complete this exercise not in the U.S. but in India, you will react much differently to the example concerning the cow. The cultural setting complicates the exercise. Hindus don't kick cows, which hold sacred status in India. In Spain, people would tend to value saving face at the moment of a car accident, even if it means a raised voice or a clenched fist. They also don't think it unseemly to urinate beside the road. There are communities where protests rather frequently take the form of blocking off a street.

Is any one of those items ethically right? It depends. Is

any one of those items wrong? It depends. In both cases it depends on culture. Within the boundaries of a cultural scene, morality is more or less understood and agreed upon. But across cultures, one can hardly predict moral preferences because communities differ in what they consider to be taboo in their management of morality. Myron W. Lustig explains the situation:

> As you can see, *value* and *culture* are inextricably linked. Each can be understood only in terms of the other because values form the basis for cultural differences. In a sense, a culture's values provide the basic set of standards and assumptions that guide thought and action. By providing its members with shared beliefs and assumptions about the "right" and "proper" ways of behaving, cultures provide the context within which individual values develop (1988, 56).

A first-time consideration of morality across cultures can be unsettling, even shocking, as though the person has opened a door—and just beyond, found a corpse. Questions arise: Are you saying that morality is relative? Are rightness and wrongness merely situational? Does this mean that I must discard my values when reacting to another culture?

Exposure to a new culture causes many people to explore value systems for the first time; discoveries often lead to reexamining the foundation of their own ethical structures. Such an inquiry is liberating for some and frightening for others, especially those in need of assurance that in a world where so much seems to cave in to relativism, there remain some stable and enduring verities. Is it inevitable that cultural studies lead to the destruction of conscience?

No, culture learning doesn't have to lead to a deterioration in values or to moral chaos. Let's look first at ethics and, specifically, how culture and ethics are related. Then I'll suggest an agenda for the further study of values across cultures.

Metaphors and frames of reference for ethical analysis

The metaphors or frames of reference we use in probing difficult issues serve to structure our thoughts about those issues. Consequently it is important to select the metaphors and frames of reference very carefully, but also, in the words of Robert Frost, "know when to get off" them (1973).

One frame of reference used in thinking about ethical issues is the etic-emic dichotomy. Lustig elaborates on the distinction. Mental programming that is "shared by all humanity" and "essentially universal," he says, comes under the rubric of etic activity. Mental programming that is formed within a specific culture and unique to it comes under the category of emic activity (1988, 55-56). A dualism of the local and the universal is thus introduced into thinking about ethical behavior. According to this dichotomy, some conduct is guided by particular situations, some by general principles. Such a dualism allows a dialogue between the two ethical sets, though it leads at times to contradiction, tension, and warfare between them. For example, within the same community there may be two ethical standards concerning the killing of a human being. One opposes killing human beings, including capital punishment for crimes committed, as immoral based on what is believed to be a universal principle. The other standard, local in origin, might support capital punishment for certain kinds of crimes even while accepting as a general proposition that killing people is immoral. Some within the community might accommodate this duality while others find the contradiction insupportable.

A different type of metaphor for analyzing ethical issues comes from systems theory. Just as a factory system may be analyzed as the operation of interlinked components, each functioning in response to messages from other components, so an ethical system may be seen as the functioning of interdependent parts. The state, schools, churches, families, and all other social institutions become components linked together. One institution's rules affect the next institution's. Further, a rule today might be changed tomorrow depending upon the influences that components of the system have on each other. Systems thinking helps one to understand ethical thought as the dynamic and ongoing result of many factors. But systems thinking has its disadvantages: a person can feel insignificant and removed from the shaping and reshaping of norms and, consequently, lack motivation to internalize existing ethical codes.

Another metaphor for ethical thought comes from the

language of structures: the foundation, the framing, the finish work. You may think of the foundation as representing the deepest and broadest dimensions of ethical consciousness, the framing as representing the organization and structure of cultural groups, and the finish work as the individual and idiosyncratic shaping of personal conscience. I prefer this metaphor and shall use it to distinguish relative ethical claims from universal ethical claims.

Foundations for ethical choice

The concept of foundation suggests something fundamental, a base upon which a thing stands. An ethical foundation, then, might represent the sense of "oughtness" that is shared by people of all times and places. This sense defies linguistic form, although people throughout history have tried to express it. One example of a universal moral imperative that forms the foundation of a system of social ethics is what has come to be known as "the golden rule": "Do unto others as you would have them do unto you." Similar concepts are expressed in various ways in many cultures. Confucius said that practicing *jen* (roughly translated as "humanism") is not to do to another person what you yourself don't want done to you. "If there's something that you don't like in the person to your right, don't pass it on to the person on your left. If there's something you don't like in the person to your left, don't pass it on to the person on your right" (Yum 1991). Two basic ethical principles of *dharma*, a Hindu code of conduct, are compassion and the avoiding of unnecessary injury to others (Koller 1982, 62). The traditional Japanese group ethic has led to what outsiders label the "I am we" formula, having to do with *kou* (filial piety), *giri* (duty), and *on* (obligation)—an ethic leading to considerable sensitivity to one's associates (Haglund 1984). Thus, one can find expressions of this comprehensive social ethic in many languages and in many different versions.

The philosopher Immanuel Kant has placed this sense into what he calls "the categorical imperative":

> Act only on that maxim which you can at the time will to be a universal law (Greene 1929, 302).

An abstract, philosophical statement of this kind may

seem somewhat irrelevant to the practical task of culture learning; however, all of us should think more about basic ethical imperatives. Elvin Hatch, for example, has argued that cultures can indeed be judged and that such assessments may be made on the basis of universal imperatives. To answer the scoffers who say that such a measuring device can't possibly be found, he has tried to identify a universal ethic for all peoples in all places. He calls his formula "humanist principles."

1. It is good to treat people well (or that we should not do one another harm)

2. People ought to enjoy a reasonable level of material existence (or conversely, that poverty, malnutrition, material discomfort, human suffering, and the like are bad) (1983, 134-37).

Hatch's "principles" on first reading seem simple, obvious, and general, and yet they have a prescriptive power concerning how people ought to act and how people ought to be treated. Upon such a foundation of universal morality, then, is built a structure of ethical consciousness. You might wish to think through what you believe the people of your own culture consider to be the crucial principles of their ethical foundation.

The framing of ethical consciousness within cultures

When you make ethical choices, it is unlikely that you will be able to trace your decision back to the philosophical base on which any given choice rests, though some people in weighing moral alternatives do think through the philosophical principles involved. More typically, people behave without consciously examining the process by which they arrived at the principles on which they are acting. If pressed, they might say they made such and such a choice because they were doing

- what was fun
- what was educational
- what was safe (or efficient or effective)
- what felt right
- what was consistent with their values

- what was approved by their religion
- what their college, travel agent, employer, supervisor wanted them to do
- what was American (or Italian or Brazilian or Indonesian)

If you pause to examine the nature of the rationale you give for your choice, you will discover a cultural apparatus encompassing it. If you do what is fun, you are conforming to what your culture has helped you define as fun. If you do what your college wants you to do, you are submitting to the influence of a social institution within the culture. If you make choices in keeping with religious principles, you pay allegiance to a culturally shaped tradition of faith and practice. If you fit your conduct to Brazilian or Indonesian patterns, you are adapting to ethnic or national entities shaped by those cultures. Whatever may be the cultural influence, you can be sure that the ethical norm has resulted from an important process that served some group of people well enough to be deemed significant and useful and right.

What are the special influences that contribute to a culture's shaping of its ethical norms? Many factors, great and small. Consider, for example, how a peoples' worldview supplies a fundamental frame of reference for all of their thinking about right and wrong. A large portion of the planet's population, for instance, sees ultimate good in terms of harmony, a belief that prevails in Eastern religions where life is understood in terms of cyclical patterns, pantheistic and immanent divinities, and quests for meaning through self-discipline. Contrast that with the worldview of an equally large portion of the population that sees ultimate good in transformation, a central belief in Western religions where life is understood in terms of a transcendent deity, a teleological design for history, and liberation through divine grace (Smart 1988). Clearly, cultural groups within each of those two larger world communities would do their ethical framing differently from each other.

But worldviews, important as they are, aren't the only shapers of ethical norms. Marshall R. Singer (1987) describes two other forces that help to form values—*environment* and *history*. Imagine how any of the following environmental factors might affect a culture and eventually help shape its values: a cold rather than a hot climate, arid rather than fertile soil, antagonistic rather than peaceful relations with neighbors.

The people of polar and tropical regions have been contrasted not just in the kinds of houses they live in, but in the openness and closedness of their human relationships. One may even build a case that the climate of southern Europe has contributed to the development of values and behaviors different from those in northern Europe. In southern Europe, doors and windows are opened. Language is expressive, gestures expansive. Emotions, ranging from anger to *amor*, are publicly proclaimed and demonstrated. In northern Europe, the colder weather drives people indoors and under wraps. Distance is measured, as are linguistic and emotional expression.

Singer illustrates how environment and history influence culture by comparing the acceptable age for marriage in the nineteenth century in Ireland (about thirty) and in India (about twelve or thirteen) and links those social codes to seemingly unrelated factors: life expectancy, food sources, and population-growth rates. He concludes:

> ...every group is confronted with environmental realities of one sort or another. Every group must deal with those realities in one way or another, or it will perish (Singer 1987, 169).

It is important to remember that one's sense of what is ethical is framed within a culture through a complex dynamic of philosophical, historical, and environmental forces.

The finish work of ethical development

As we have seen, the foundations for ethical choice may be seen to be as deep and wide as human consciousness. All over the world and all through history human beings have upheld what they consider to be moral verities. These moral verities are the foundation upon which the construction of ethical consciousness builds, within the context of a culture, by framing up certain local or group understandings. At one time fathers and mothers expressed these understandings in the memorable words, "Now remember who you are." Good character is acknowledged by a communal seal of approval.

The finish work in this construction project is of a more

personal nature. An individual lives by a conscience that is shaped by the imprint of genetic makeup, the idiosyncrasies of personality, the reinforcement of personal experience, and the consequence of personal choice.

To locate this personal function within the larger construct, consider an anecdote. Kermit Eby, in an essay on personal integrity (1955), tells of Rabbi Joseph the builder: One day when he was working high on a scaffolding, his opinion was sought on a certain matter. The questioner, standing below, called up to him, "Come down. I want to ask you something." Rabbi Joseph replied, "I cannot come down because I was hired by the day."

In this story, one may see the whole of this ethical structure in relief. First is the foundation work in ethical consciousness—Rabbi Joseph was honoring his belief in what he considered a universal principle, that a good life depends upon hard work. Just as we expect others to do their share of work, so we do ours. Second, one may see what we have been calling the framing work in ethical development—the Jewish communal understanding that makes the rabbi a respected person to ask for counsel and that supports an esteem for conscientious work habits. Third, the rabbi puts his own personal touch upon the matter—taking a work contract so seriously that he single-mindedly works at fulfilling the contract, avoiding all distractions.

Like Rabbi Joseph, we all develop a unique and idiosyncratic conscience. We do it as we try to make sense of life, prove our genuineness, tell the truth, and seek peace. We do it as we try to avoid wrongdoing and the loss of self-respect.

Because of the personal nature of this finish work, people go about it in different ways. To be sure, most of us aren't aware of the ongoing process of making and remaking our ethical commitments. We work with what we've been given and with what we've got. On occasion, we become deliberate about ethical choices; then, we each use a privately held recipe of subjective feelings and beliefs mixed with another powerful ingredient—the real world. Thus we come up with a newly educated personal conscience.

With this perspective on values in mind, it should be clear that intercultural experience and culture learning do not have to lead you into a morass of cultural relativity. Instead, by throwing light on your own values and bringing them into sharper focus, the intercultural experience offers you the opportunity to enhance, elaborate, and strengthen the value system you have inherited and developed over the course of your life.

Applications for culture learners

The study of values can expand the range and the depth of your culture learning. Examining your values calls for intellectual processing—vigorous brain work of the most demanding kind. But there is also the emotional side to the study, because values touch our feelings. Values also govern action and can be understood only when put into practice. Here are seven suggestions to help you process values intellectually, emotionally, and behaviorally. Some of them are keyed to related guides, some of them refer you to other literature.

1. *Reacquaint yourself with your own culture's values while you are in a new cultural setting where values seem to differ from yours.* To help in this, we suggest an exercise having to do with political values, adapted from work by David Bender (1989). Read over the following list of fourteen personal and political values:

Your Values	American Values	Host Culture Values
financial security		
freedom of speech		
equality of opportunity		
self-reliance		
loyalty to country		
tolerance of others		
freedom of religion		
individual initiative		
right to private property		
government by law		
concern for the underdog		
fair play		
justice		
social order and stability		

Now, do three things with Bender's list: (1) Rank order each of the items according to how important they are to you personally. In other words, place a 1 after the item you value most highly, a 2 after the next one, and so forth. (2) Rank order each of the values according to how important you think they are to most Americans. (3) Rank order the values the way you suppose the people of your host culture would.

This exercise, limited to just one small group of the ideas we hold dear, can help you retrieve from your subconscious some of the values you take for granted. You might try the same exercise in social, educational, and religious values and the like. Record what you consider to be your core values.

An especially potent way to explore comparative values is to do this exercise with one or more members of your host culture, asking them to add values of importance to them which do not appear on the list. Discussing the results with an open mind and nonjudgmentally will result in significant and often surprising discoveries about your host culture's values.

2. *Be aware of how your own value system might constitute a set of blinders that limit or modify how you see the values of others.* To help you in this task, refer to a study made by Geert H. Hofstede (1984) of four selected value dimensions using data from 116,000 respondents in forty countries. He compared how these values were rank ordered in each country. The comparison is quite revealing for citizens of those countries (in which the United States is included) and can be found in Guide 8.

3. *Find structured ways to identify your host culture's values.* Values, unlike laws, aren't written for people to read and memorize. They are hidden...until people act. The casual tourist is not likely to be able to determine what a peoples' value system is. To help you intercept the values, I recommend the work of Milton Rokeach (1960, 1968, 1973, 1984). Rokeach developed a scheme by which values can be identified, examined, and better understood.

4. *Learn about the formation of their values.* This is a difficult task. One way you might approach it is to find examples in your host culture of what Singer (1987) calls the basic influences on perception: (1) physical determinants, (2) environmental determinants, (3) learned determinants, (4) attitudes and values, and (5) belief systems. Then think about whether the examples you come up with do indeed serve as molders and shapers of the way your hosts live. To help you do this, Guide 9 provides a list of culture contrasts developed by Sondra Thiederman (1991) designed to stimulate your thinking about how and why values differ.

5. *Don't judge your host culture's value system prematurely.* There has been considerable discussion about the validity of an outsider evaluating a culture. Cultural relativists, such as Melville J. Herskovits (1972), argue that a culture's value system is indigenous, arrived at through an historical process that gives it inherent authenticity. It is unlikely that an outsider, making judgments about it, will be able to appreciate fully the context, the culture's history, and the fact that it constitutes an integrated and logical system. On the other hand, Elvin Hatch (1983) thinks the relativists have been too hesitant to use humanistic principles in assessing whether a peoples' values ultimately lead to well-being. The controversy serves to caution us against quick and ethnocentric judgments of others.

 A good place to explore your host culture's values is in a small discussion group where you can consider together the wisdom of being a cultural evaluator in regard to any given value.

6. *Explore the moral ambiguities in your host's values through the art of the culture.* The local framing of morality will surely offer you what seem to be inconsistencies and contradictions. Social mores confuse and provoke even the people who accept them as part of their culture. Use the culture's arts to help you clarify your thoughts about these ambiguities. Make a habit of going to the theater to see local plays. I

have found that drama kneads the moral sense, working it over for an audience to contemplate. Theater is a microcosm of life because life is a stage where characters live out the consequences of their moral choices. Films and novels deal with values in a similar way.

7. *Use a journal to refine your thinking about the development of your own values and moral perspectives.* Travelers and sojourners who get involved in discussions of universal and relative values are forced to think about the origins of their own ethical structures and to place under new examination the moral health of the community back home. For thoughtful people, the clarification of their own values is an ongoing activity, sometimes characterized by struggle, sometimes characterized by slow percolation. A journal accommodates both.

Sojourners know that new experience becomes new knowledge, and new knowledge demands disciplined thought and action.

Chapter 6

Guides to the
Culture-Learning Process

Guide 1

Noting Differences

Raymonde Carroll, in *Cultural Misunderstandings: The French/
American Experience* (1988), says that although many French
and Americans perceive each other as quite similar, there
are in fact profound differences which often cause break-
downs in their relationships—issues such as privacy, self-
disclosure, and appropriate topics and styles of conversation. French and American perceptions of each other and of
social situations lead the participants into faulty predictions.
Carroll, like most cultural scholars, urges a careful detection
and sorting out of those differences, followed by a revision
of the perceptions.

Instead of leaping blindly over cultural differences—pre-
tending they aren't there or trying to minimize their significance—you need to learn to take a good look at them. *Seeing*
cultural differences will lead you to an understanding of them
which will foster improved cross-cultural communication.

Here is an exercise to help you perceive cultural differences more accurately. It leads you through three stages: identifying differences, analyzing them, and enhancing communication through your new understanding of the differences. Modify the exercise to fit your situation.

Select a cultural behavior to observe

We suggest you focus upon a single behavior, so that your observations can be relatively specific. Select a behavior from this list of nineteen, or let the list lead you to another of more interest or relevance to you.

- playing (as in athletics)
- adorning one's body
- cooking
- courting, dating
- dancing
- feasting, celebrating
- praying, worshipping
- participating in a funeral or other death rite
- driving
- gesturing
- giving gifts
- competing for attention, for power, etc.
- greeting other people
- maintaining cleanliness (food, house, car, person)
- singing, whistling, making music
- working
- getting medical care
- laughing, joking, playing pranks
- studying

Let us suppose that you select the final one, studying, as the behavior you wish to observe.

Identify the differences

Here is a scheme to use. It is designed for an American student in the People's Republic of China trying to identify the differences between her study habits and the study habits of

Chinese youth her age. You, of course, would make the comparison with a student in your host culture.

A scheme for identifying differences in study habits

Lead questions	American student	Chinese student
study where? library, dorm, classroom, home, elsewhere	_____	_____
study when? days of week, time of day, hours at a stretch	_____	_____
study what? assignments, books, notes, labs, videos, projects	_____	_____
study how? desk, chair, lamp, bed, phone, radio, food, typewriters, computers, alone, with others, memorizing, writing, active, passive	_____	_____
study why? grades, job, family expectations, personal advancement	_____	_____

The number of cited differences could grow quite long. But what do the differences add up to? They are not merely curiosities; they are the stuff of culture learning and call for analysis.

Analyze the differences

Here's a work sheet to direct your analysis. We will continue using the hypothetical case of study habits, expecting you to adapt the work sheet to your subject. On the left side of the work sheet are some key assumptions that govern cultural behaviors. How do these kinds of cultural assumptions shape specific behaviors in your own culture and in your host culture? The task is to examine the descriptions you wrote in the above scheme in the context of each of the assumptions listed. Do the study behaviors, American or Chinese, reveal themselves as a manifestation of these assumptions? How? What is the significance or relevance to you as a culture learner, as a guest in the society, as one who must adapt to different cultural norms? As you jot down your notes you will need more space, probably several pages from your journal.

A work sheet on the relationship
of behavior and cultural assumptions

Cultural assumptions*	American study habits	Chinese study habits
Perception of oneself: assumptions about how one identifies self in relation to others, in regard to self-concept, self-respect	_____	_____
Personal responsibility: assumptions about the tasks or obligations an individual is expected to do independently	_____	_____
Concept of time: assumptions about past, present, future orientations; about time as a commodity; about use and misuse of time	_____	_____
Use of space: assumptions about quantity and quality of space,		

Cultural assumptions*	American study habits	Chinese study habits
about exclusive and inclusive space, about maximum and minimum space	_____	_____
Desire for achievement: assumptions about motivation, desire, advancement, obligation	_____	_____
Competition and affiliation: assumptions about cooperative and noncooperative, individualistic and group-oriented actions	_____	_____
Equality, status: assumptions about class, rank, dominance, and nondominance	_____	_____
Work and play: assumptions about the unity or separation of work and play	_____	_____

*The items are adapted from Stewart and Bennett, *American Cultural Patterns: A Cross-Cultural Perspective,* 1991.

Enhancing cross-cultural communication through an awareness of cultural differences

It is easier to identify differences than to detect the subtle cultural assumptions that support them. Even more difficult is understanding the variants well enough to communicate better across cultures. For example, I may discover that my hosts differ from me in how they use their study time, and I may come to the point of seeing a relationship between their study behavior and their larger cultural assumptions about achievement, but I may still have a long way to go before I can fully work out the most desirable relationships between *their* assumptions, perceptions, and behaviors and my own.

Most important, an eyes-open study of differences can help you sharpen your perceptions of strangers, leading you to make more accurate generalizations about them. Second, you can draw mental pictures of them that come closer to whom they really are, rather than pictures based on flawed stereotypes. Third, as you consider the differences that distinguish them from you, you may become a better predictor of their conduct, because their behaviors will begin to be more consistent with what you noticed on previous occasions. Fourth, these apparent differences may serve as paths by which to find your way into their culture, where you can discover what is concealed from the outsider. Finally, this rigorous study may help you to shape your behavior to be more compatible with theirs, without compromising who you are.

Interpreting Nonverbal Cues

We use gesture, posture, space, time, and many other subtle nonverbal cues to convey meaning. This guide explores in greater detail the ways in which people communicate through their use of body language.

Carey Quan Gelernter, a newspaper columnist for *The Seattle Times,* writes, "If you are Americans chatting in a coffee shop, you probably touch each other twice an hour. If you are English, you probably don't touch each other at all. If you're French, you touch 110 times an hour." This is a humorous example of the relevance of body language. The person who frequently crosses cultural boundaries must learn to intercept, interpret, and use this type of nonverbal cue if communication is to be efficient and effective.

Observing nonverbal actions
Stop, look, listen, and then try to answer these questions about nonverbal actions in your host country.

1. Direct your attention to the way family members in your host country give nonverbal cues to each other. How does a parent beckon a child? How does a child beg for others' attention? How does a child tell a sibling to "stop it!" How does a teenager show the wish for independence? How does a parent indicate that the fooling around has gone far enough? Which of these cues are used in the same way you use them at home? Which are different?

2. Consider basic life functions. What are some of the nonverbal ways people refer to eating? To sleeping? To drinking? To having to use a rest room? To bathing? To primping? Think about the faculties they employ in conveying these cues: the face and eyes, hands, shoulders and back, hips and legs.

3. Find examples of how people describe other people, for example:

   • "The child is big for his age...maybe this big." (In some cultures, for animals, hand extended, palm down; for children, hand extended, palm down but wrist crooked upward)

   • "She is very wealthy, and she wants you to know it." (A slight, quick twitting of nose or a thumb quickly rubbing two fingers)

   • "He is very lazy" (Head resting on palm) or "He's a go-getter." (Snap, snap of fingers)

   • "She is devious" (Raised eyebrows, tilt of head or a quick sway of hips) or "She is a saint." (Hands folded in prayer or a cross traced across the heart)

   • "That child is stupid" (A twirling finger pointed to side of forehead) or "She is terribly bright." (Eyebrows up, eyes open wide)

   • "He takes to the bottle a lot." (Thumb and little finger raised, thumb pointed to mouth, wrist wriggled back and forth)

   As you observe these nonverbal cues, can you also detect the ways that the people add nonverbal emphases to what they are conveying, such as making the gesture twice, or using two gestures that reinforce each other, or using both nonverbal and verbal means to say it?

4. Look for nonverbal communication in public. If a person is waiting in a long line in a bank, how does he or she express displeasure at the waiting? How does one hail a taxi? How do fans at a ball game tell the referee that a call was wrong? If you have traveled in more than one foreign country, indicate the similarities and differences in the nonverbal cues.

5. As people pass on a sidewalk, is there eye contact? Do both men and women make eye contact? At what distance? For how long? In the United States would you answer those questions similarly in (a) your hometown, (b) a southern city, (c) downtown New York?

6. Cultural observers would say that the use of and the functions and sanctions related to staring vary greatly from culture to culture. Is staring acceptable? By whom? Toward what? Is staring ever considered an illness? A manner of admiring? A way to attract attention? Do parents scold children for staring? You may have to chat with a cultural informant or interpreter to help you understand local staring customs.

I like, I dislike—nonverbally

Now try a more focused study. Recall only the nonverbal cues that convey that people in your host culture like or dislike something. For each of those two meanings, find at least one nonverbal cue, and write it down.

categories of nonverbal cues	host culture cues of liking	host culture cues of disliking
eyes	_____	_____
eyebrows	_____	_____
face	_____	_____
tilt of head	_____	_____
hands	_____	_____
posture	_____	_____
space	_____	_____

categories of nonverbal cues	host culture cues of liking	host culture cues of disliking
time	_____	_____
pitch of voice	_____	_____
tone of voice	_____	_____

Here's an exercise that is normally done in a group, though one could do it informally with a friend or two, with one's own family (if you're abroad together), or even with the host family if you have established a very trusting relationship. In fact, it would be especially enlightening to do this exercise with a bi- or multicultural group.

With whatever group you have assembled, take turns in role playing one of the nonverbal communication acts listed above. It may be a facial expression, a gesture, a use of space, an expression of speed or tone or punctuation. The performer should indicate when and where the act was observed. As time permits, interpret the possible nuances of "I like" or "I dislike" found in each nonverbal act.

On the basis of what you learn from these nonverbal cues, you may try to construct a larger system about liking and disliking that could not be understood only from words. What do they like? Whom do they like? What do they dislike? Whom do they dislike?

While this exercise focuses on *like-dislike,* you might wish to study other messages coded nonverbally by your host culture. Examples:

- I am intelligent; I am stupid.
- I am submissive; I am powerful.
- I am wealthy; I am poor.
- I am a follower; I am a leader.
- I am conservative; I am progressive.

This guide should be a reminder that you, too, engage in nonverbal communication. Some of the cues you give off are American-made; some are of your own making. People in your host country are reading them, sometimes correctly and sometimes incorrectly. In your journal you might wish to inventory your more obvious and frequently used nonverbal cues and assess how accurately they are being interpreted by your hosts. Should you change some of your nonverbal signing in order to be a better intercultural communicator? Should you try to modify or use additional ways to reinforce your nonverbal communication so that people will understand you better?

Interactions

This guide will help you sharpen your observation skills as you attempt to understand better the nature of personal interaction and patterns of communication among your hosts. Interactions take place constantly, providing a wealth of social and cultural information. Although you may still be a beginner in speaking the language, you can learn a great deal about styles of interaction simply by watching people in conversation, listening for volume, tone and stress in their speech, and noticing their gestures and the social distance they maintain. You should also be ready to begin making some inferences about the motivations and attitudes behind the interactions—a light cross-cultural dose of social psychology. Understanding how people interact is critical to getting beneath the surface in cross-cultural relationships and to the effective pursuit of culture learning.

Who interacts with whom? When? How?

1. What is typically the happiest part of the day in the house? The most tense?

2. When does the family spend time together? Doing what? Is anyone excluded?

3. Do all members interact in equal freedom with father? Mother?

4. How do they react to grandparents? Uncles and aunts? Cousins?

5. Within the family setting, who touches whom? Where? On what occasions?

6. Do all members interact with the maid? The gardener? The driver? Are these workers treated as family members or employees?

7. Do neighborhood children play in your host's house? If not, where do they play?

8. Do relatives drop in unannounced? Does your family meet relatives elsewhere? Where do they live? How often do they meet? Describe the events.

9. Do friends stop in after school?

10. During the day, do neighbor women get together? Where? When?

11. Do neighbor men interact? When? Where?

12. Does your family have dinner parties? Sunday guests? Who do the guests tend to be? What do they talk about? What do they do?

13. Is your family a member of a close-knit small group?

14. Does your family regularly socialize at a club? Does your family ever eat out? Go to movies? Attend athletic contests? Who goes? With whom?

Inside the house

Describe in detail the words and gestures used by your family upon

- seeing each other in the morning
- leaving for work or school

- going to bed
- saying good-byes (for an extended absence)
- showing approval
- indicating displeasure
- apologizing
- getting angry

Behavior toward the outsider

1. How does your host family answer the phone?
2. If a wrong number is called, how do they respond?
3. How do they react when a food huckster knocks at the door? A bill collector? A beggar?
4. To whom would your family give a gift? On what occasions?
5. Whom in the family or neighborhood do they tease?
6. Are there feelings against some residents of your immediate neighborhood? Why?
7. How does at-home behavior change when the people are in a car? At an athletic event? At the market? At a family gathering?

Making some generalizations

1. As you think about the interactions of your host family, you might profitably compare and contrast them with your own family. On the scales below, place an x at the appropriate place on each continuum to describe your host family, and an o at the appropriate place to describe your own family.

```
private ........................................ public
active .......................................... passive
formal ......................................... informal
authoritarian ............................ democratic
extended ..................................... nuclear
hospitable ................................... reserved
driven ......................................... casual
class-conscious ......................... egalitarian
tolerant ....................................... prejudiced
political ...................................... apolitical
```

communal .... private
generous .... tightfisted
gossipy .... tight-lipped

Are there other characteristics that should be added to this list?

2. In your journal write out a profile of your host culture using this exercise and other exercises, experiences, and readings. Cover such things as customary behaviors, values and assumptions, expectations, and patterns of communication and interaction. Compare and contrast them with your own cultural characteristics and then record how you feel about the similarities and differences.

Naming Your Cucarachas

At the beginning of a stay overseas, especially if you are located in or near the tropical zones, you may make a quick acquaintance with *cucarachas* (cockroaches). So startling may this encounter be—in kitchen, bedroom, bathroom, or shoe— that your conversations, letters, and memories of the sojourn abroad may be populated, even infested, by cucarachas.

But international living is more than a cucaracha. Away from home there are worlds to explore, not the least of which is the grandeur of the human spirit of people in other cultures. Isn't it curious that so many of our thoughts and words have to do with the creepies and crawlies of our international environments?

A project

Here is an exercise to help you transcend your preoccupation with your own cucarachas. Throughout the first weeks of your term, set aside some time to identify the petty irritants and pestilences you've encountered. Name each one. Refine its shape and size and place in your universe. Then release it, while releasing yourself from its domination.

To help you get started, I'm listing here some cucarachas that travelers and new residents overseas have named in group sessions:

- cockroaches, of course
- spiders, bats, snakes, and slugs
- mondongo soup (stomach and intestine pieces), vertebra soup, rice soup
- cold showers
- macho men, holy men, overbearing men
- toilet paper that's not to be thrown in the toilet
- squatter toilets
- wet shoes, wet clothes, broken umbrellas
- local time (late as usual); hyperpunctuality
- littered streets, littered parks, littered lots
- fussy mothers, demanding fathers, 9:30 P.M. curfews
- crowded, broken, noisy buses
- beggars, street urchins, thieves
- indefinite street directions, unclear street signs
- males' unbuttoned shirts, females' tight dresses
- potholes, rude drivers, bicycle congestion
- smiling faces, bows, unresponsiveness
- spoiled children, doting parents
- evening TV serials, loud tapes
- "theft" of clothing and personal items
- tight spaces, small restaurants, crowded alleys
- rigid social rules, formalized courtesies, excessive rituals

- absence of wastebaskets
- rudeness toward maids, migrants, or Gypsies
- diesel smoke, air horns, motorcycle noise
- rules on footwear, skirts, slacks, and jackets
- treatment of animals on the street
- teasing of retarded or handicapped people
- soccer fervor (violence), bullbaiting
- formalities of the educational system

Questions for discussion

1. Which of your cucarachas are frightening? Life-threatening? Disgusting? Pathetic? Humorous?

2. What characterizes your cucarachas? Are they natural phenomena, such as flora and fauna? Are they manufactured? Are their customs alien to you? Are they the result of an economic situation? Political or religious orientation?

3. In what way is your list different from your traveling companions' lists? Does your own personality help to determine what you consider to be a cucaracha?

4. Which of the cucarachas can be removed from your presence? Which of them will you have to put up with?

5. To survive in the presence of those cucarachas that won't go away, what preparations or precautions or dispositions would help you?

There is another angle from which to consider cucarachas. One day as a group of my students were recovering from cucarachas, someone wondered about the experience of foreign residents and students in the United States. Do they too face cucarachas? What are the bugs or beasts that break the confidence of Asians or Africans who find our culture strange? Are these sojourners assisted in any way to name their cucarachas and to transcend them? What might we native sons and daughters learn about ourselves from their lists? We bring the subject up in all our groups now.

If you're by yourself rather than with a group, mull it over and jot down some notes in your journal if so inspired. This is also a good subject for discussion with a friend or even a host culture informant you've gotten close to. Later, if you are in a group of local residents who have lived in the United States, bring up the question of what their cucarachas were.

Learning the "isms"

A lecturer, upon learning that a group of us had just arrived in his country, gave us a gracious welcome and then said, "If you want to become acquainted with this country quickly and significantly, learn our 'isms'."

His counsel has proven to be wise. "Ism" words, it turns out, begin as private conditions or individual actions which ultimately become a broad social phenomenon or movement or a widely held belief. An idea becomes an ideology, an inspiration, a religion, a personal problem, a social blight, a method, a way of being, a personal preference, a corporate mentality. In other words, an "ism" is a personal entity that has spread out and become institutionalized by society. According to the lecturer, the "isms" can be a window through which to view people defining their world and their role in it.

Consider a relatively recent "ism": feminism. I do not know when the word was first used; the *Oxford English Dictionary* documents citings of the terms "feminism" and "feminist" in the 1890s. But feminism was not in common (that is, popular) usage when Betty Friedan published *The Feminine Mystique* in 1963. She and a few other women were keeping alive a sensibility about what it meant to be female. The book enjoyed a wide readership. Its ideas stimulated the thinking and emotions of Americans and contributed significantly to feminism becoming a social movement, a critical perspective, a political persuasion, and an expanded concept of the meaning of the word "woman." To understand contemporary society in the United States, Canada, and Western Europe, one needs to comprehend the nature of feminism.

Most of the "isms" we are familiar with are far older than feminism, and more universal. (Perhaps in time, feminism as an "ism" will be universal.) Name five of the most important "isms" in your life and thought. Look at the list below. Are your "isms" on it? Does the list include "isms" which hadn't come to mind but which you might want to substitute for ones on your list? How many on the list can you define without retreating to the dictionary? Are there "isms" you've encountered in your host country that are unique to it and/or that you've never heard of before?

A list of "isms"

name **definition**

agnosticism _____

alcoholism _____

Buddhism _____

capitalism _____

Catholicism _____

chauvinism _____

collectivism _____

colonialism _____

commercialism _____

Confucianism _____

conservatism _____

consumerism _____

feminism _____

hedonism _____

individualism _____

name	definition
industrialism	_____
institutionalism	_____
intellectualism	_____
internationalism	_____
isolationism	_____
Judaism	_____
machismo (macho-ism)	_____
parochialism	_____
professionalism	_____
progressivism	_____
Protestantism	_____
Puritanism	_____
racism	_____
regionalism	_____
sexism	_____
socialism	_____
spiritualism	_____

Now use the "isms" as instruments in defining and exploring culture, that is, as part of the process of culture learning.

1. Identify five "isms" that are crucial to defining your home culture.

2. Identify five "isms" that would be considered contrary or antagonistic to the dominant "ism" of your home culture.

3. Identify (ask a cultural interpreter if necessary) five "isms" that are an integral part of the host culture. Take care to define the terms fully. Try to discover how these terms represent subconscious understandings, collective thinking, political and economic movements, or philosophical persuasions. How does the force of these "isms" affect the way you will live in this country?

4. Identify five "isms" you feel would be contrary or antagonistic to your host culture.

5. Compare the "isms" you've identified for home and

host cultures. Which are similar, which divergent? What are the implications for intercultural communication and cross-cultural interaction? How can you use this knowledge to facilitate your ability to communicate and adapt?

Dancing Their Rhythms, Telling Their Time

Several students from India came to class at my college one day to talk to us and help us understand the long-standing and complex love-hate relationship between the Indians and the British, illustrated so vividly in E. M. Forster's novel (and film) *A Passage to India.* When the Indian students were asked to identify sources of the tension, one of them replied almost without thinking, "IST—India Standard Time." She went on to explain that the sense of time that Indians live by is totally perplexing to the British.

If the British had come to terms with India's sense of time, enough to regard it as an authentic expression of what it means to be Indian instead of stereotyping Indians as an ignorant people for whom time didn't matter, the history of their relationship might have been different. That, of course, is a gross generalization, but there is a kernel of truth in it.

In your new home, the cultural clocks will confound you at least to some degree—more so in some cultures than others. There are cultures in which time seems almost irrelevant or, at least, its management haphazard. Don't be fooled, however. No matter how it appears, every culture has a clearly defined and understood sense of time which, despite your frustration (if that's what you feel), offers a fruitful context for culture learning.

Time frames

All cultures have time frames—that is, the units that define the time limits of a function. Always keep in mind that those frames differ from culture to culture.

Begin by identifying some time frames that you regularly use:

- a second ("just a sec"); a minute ("I'll be ready in a minute")
- a commercial break, a coffee break
- being on time
- mealtime, a good night's sleep
- the 40-hour week, sick days, vacation
- the holiday season
- the school year, the fiscal year, the decade

The time frames of your host culture might be strange to you. In many Asian cultures, the time frames tend to be larger or longer, centuries in length, and slower moving. In Latin America and among some Native American cultures, you will probably encounter time frames that aren't clock units: an event begins "when the time is right."

You may also become aware of large time dividers—before or after Jesus Christ, before or after Mohammed, before or after a regime, before or after an economic or a natural disaster.

To get you started in your study of time frames, try to identify your host culture's time frames in the life span. American time frames are suggested on the left side; complete the right side for your host culture. You might want to consult your cultural informant in doing this exercise. Some of the categories on the left won't appear on the right. The right side may have categories not found on the left.

Time frames in the life span

in the United States	in my host culture
a baby (birth-3 years)	_____
preschooler (4-5 years)	_____
child (6-10 or 11 years)	_____
early adolescent (11-13 years)	_____
teenager (14-18)	_____
driving age (16 ff.)	_____
"R"-rated movie age (18 ff.)	_____
drinking age (18 or 21 ff.)	_____
legal adult (21 ff.)	_____
marriageable (ambiguous)	_____
young adult (21-35)	_____
middle adult (36-55)	_____
older adult (56-65)	_____
senior citizen (66 ff.)	_____

Rhythms

All cultures have rhythms. Fast and slow. Back and forth. On and off. Ebb and flow. Up and down. Begin to study rhythms by identifying some of the rhythms in your home culture. Can you define those rhythms in terms of moods, energy levels, clothing styles, activities? Day and night? Workweek and weekend? School year and vacation? Cold months and hot months?

In your host culture, the source of the rhythms may have to do with phenomena you aren't tuned in to. Is there a rhythm suggested by rainy and dry seasons or some other weather pattern? By Holy Week or some other religious calendar? By planting and harvesting, or some other factor of subsistence? By Independence Day or some other event of history? By the sports season? Or the season when fishing is good? Or the season of concerts, ballets, operas, and plays?

With the help of friends, cultural interpreters, or your host family, try to identify an activity or a set of activities that can be described in terms of the rhythms listed below. For example, at the beginning of the week as people arrive at work, the activities tend to be at the "flow" end of the first continuum. On Friday afternoons, the activities ebb. In most cultures, a wedding begins at the formal end of the second continuum and, as the day progresses, moves toward the informal. "On" and "off" may be illustrated in the performing arts. Plays, concerts, and films are showing or they aren't—they're on tonight or off. The farmer's market is an activity of the day, usually the morning, whereas the town's soccer games (now that there are lights) may be played at night.

Rhythms and events

ebb	flow
formal	informal
on	off
day	night
loud	quiet
wet	dry
sad	happy
profane	sacred
fast	slow
work	play

Time contexts

Time is manifest in situations. You can begin examining the contexts of time by thinking of events in your own culture—let's say at home, at school, and at work—when it is appropriate to go slowly or when activities are expected to speed up. The context helps to define the characteristic time takes on.

Turn now to your host culture. Try to recall the places you've been: downtown, in the countryside, at the doctor's office, or at sporting events. Locate places where people of your host culture

- can expect to wait five minutes
- can expect to wait twenty minutes
- won't be surprised if they have to wait an hour
- will protest if they have to wait at all

Can you find occasions when most people want the clock to move fast? When they want time to stand still?

Compare two contexts and the activities and sense of time that characterize each:

Monday morning at 6:30 with Sunday morning at 9:30

Saturday night at 8:30 with Tuesday noon

List the differences. Which has a quicker pace? Why? How do the different contexts affect behavior? Would the differences be the same at home? Can you make your own internal clock tick to the context you find yourself in?

Time manipulations

You come from a culture that believes in controlling nature and manipulating time. It defies the seasons with central heating and air conditioning. It erases time and distance with high-speed transportation. It invented "high technology" out of a need and thirst for labor- and time-saving devices like washing machines, vacuum cleaners, and a whole array of common appliances. It created fast foods and drive-up windows to save time and employs electronic gadgets to manipulate time in reverse and produce slow motion.

Not all people manage time in this way. Even other high-tech societies vary in some degree from the United States. And in still other cultures where modern technology has not yet become ascendant, people are able to blend into contrasting slow and fast flows of time without trying to modify them. Accounts are told of commercial fishermen who may wait for days, seemingly doing nothing but passing the time. But when the schools of fish approach, these same people might work three or four days without a break. I recall hosts who laughed at American students who ran through the rain so that they wouldn't get so wet; in contrast, the hosts stopped their activities and waited for the rain to pass.

To help you perceive and understand the presence of time manipulation, you might wish to identify examples for each of the following:

natural time	artificial time
using the sun	using the clock
showing one's age	concealing one's age
going at a comfortable pace	going fast or slow
living in the present	living for the future
being unaware of clocks	watching the clock
accommodating circumstances	manipulating circumstances

Time and values

Begin to search for connections between time and values. A variety of questions may open this door. When is it good to be speedy? When is it bad? Can you find an occasion when a person offends by staying too long? In contrast, what about the person who gives some extended time to a neighbor in need?

How does development theory prejudice the discussion about time by expecting people to be manipulators of time? Does an individual's "time of life" (age) imply certain restrictions or privileges? Is God (or divine sanction) associated in any way with time?

Identify occasions when a person's use of time is considered to be

- reckless
- wasteful
- compassionate
- prudent
- cunning
- thoughtless

Would they be judged the same in your host culture as in your home culture? Become aware of how people who manipulate time and people who accommodate time make negative judgments about each other. Monitor your own attitudes: are you more critical of the person who manipulates time or the person who lives by natural time?

Guide 7

Dealing with Culture Shock

Kalvero Oberg's presentation to the Women's Club of Rio de Janeiro on August 3, 1954, was probably not the first time that the words "culture shock" were used. But that lecture (see Oberg 1960) has become a classic beginning to the formal investigations into this "occupational disease of people who have been transplanted abroad."

Culture shock is a term widely known and a condition widely feared. It involves emotional and physical responses to "the accumulated stresses and strains which stem from being forced to meet one's everyday needs in unfamiliar ways" (Brislin 1981, 13).

But culture shock isn't all bad, as you will discover.

This guide introduces this important topic in outline form, based in part on Richard W. Brislin's *Cross-Cultural Encounters* (1981). As you read, we encourage you to jot down your own personal experiences and observations in your journal. Note whether you've had the experiences described or if a friend has—or, indeed, speculate on why you haven't, if such is the case. Have they affected you? How? If they've had a negative effect, what can you do to counteract or help a friend counteract it?

Stages to cultural adjustment

Oberg suggested that culture shock and cross-cultural adjustment progress through four stages that I am expressing in the metaphor of terrain:

1. the honeymoon on the mountain, elevated emotion from lots of unusual stimuli, exhilaration from novel activities, a heady sense of having done yourself proud in getting to another culture, early fascination with all the sights and sounds

2. loneliness in the valley, the plummet into harsh reality, confusion and frustration, fatigue, emotions turning from buoyancy to heaviness, hostile and aggressive attitude toward the hosts and assertion of cultural superiority, or undiscriminating approval of hosts and denigration of yourself and your own culture

3. the slow climb, getting yourself acclimated, searching for solutions to maladjustments, meeting people, becoming involved, learning new procedures, establishing new patterns, adapting to new ways

4. the integration partway up the mountains from the valley—putting things together, accepting the highs and the lows of the new culture, redefining your own cultural borders, becoming a part of the host culture and comfortably traversing its various terrains

This is essentially a linear progression and is somewhat oversimplified. Culture shock, culture fascination, culture fatigue, and cultural integration often occur in haphazard order—sometimes in cycles, sometimes in conjunction with each other. Some of my own more painful regressions and depressions occurred in my fifth year abroad. Nonetheless, Oberg did us a service in showing how one might deal with cultural adjustment in a systematic way.

Take a moment to answer the following questions in your journal: How do your experiences fit into the above stages? How do they differ? Can you think of specific examples for each stage? What stage are you at right now?

Symptoms of culture shock

Oberg listed a number of the symptoms of culture shock. Other writers and researchers have added to the list. Here are some of the most commonly identified symptoms. Have you or anyone you know experienced any of them?

- fatigue, discomfort, generalized frustration
- a feeling of helplessness, the inability to cope with the demands of the day
- excessive preoccupation with personal cleanliness, manifested in worries about food, drinking water, bedding, and dirt in one's surroundings; excessive washing of hands; preoccupation with personal health, minor pains, skin rashes, etc.
- fear of physical contact with attendants or servants; excessive fear of being cheated, robbed, or injured resulting in negative feelings toward hosts; and a refusal to learn their language or practice their common courtesies
- irritability at slight provocations, criticisms; fits of anger over delays and other minor frustrations
- loneliness; a need to meet others, but a reluctance to let them see your sorry emotional state
- a strong desire to interact with, and be dependent upon, long-term residents of your own nationality
- a terrible longing for home, for letters, for home cooking; staring absentmindedly; being disengaged from the present; in some cases, the active desire to return home
- loss of inventiveness, spontaneity and flexibility, so that work declines in quality
- difficulty in communicating feelings to others

Undoubtedly you will feel some jolts as you try to get along in a strange culture, but you might not experience any of the above feelings with any severity. Your telltale signs of stress may be evidenced in milder ways: a preoccupation with sending and receiving letters, a fear of getting lost, anxiety over language demands, wanting to spend evenings and weekends with other Americans, recurrence of nagging emotional distress, change in appetite, and, of course, simple homesickness.

Identify symptoms of culture shock you have observed in yourself or others and describe, interpret, and evaluate them in your journal.

Causes of culture shock

A person experiencing culture shock will rarely be able to state the exact cause of the problem. Objective researchers who have explored the phenomenon refer most often to these causes:

- situational factors such as food, housing, climate, transportation, neighbors, etc., and the degree to which they are different from similar situations at home or from what you expected they would be
- the presence of structure where you don't want it and the lack of structure where you need it
- similarly, the presence or absence of time constraints (not enough time for some things, too much time for others)
- the lack of a niche (no place where you fit just right)
- the absence of role models
- the lack of meaningful work (an unclear job assignment, too many employees to do the job or not enough employees)
- increased ambiguity and uncertainty that makes it impossible to predict what is likely to happen next
- questions about your personal competence (self-doubt)
- deprivation of identity reinforcements

The positive results of culture shock

From the perspective of cross-cultural adjustment and adaptation, culture shock urges you to come to grips with its causes and to develop more effective ways of coping and accomplishing your aims in being abroad. It pushes you in the direction of culture learning and cross-cultural adjustment. Recall Milton J. Bennett's developmental model of intercultural sensitivity. Culture shock is a stimulus to move along the culture-learning continuum from ethnocentrism to multiculturalism. Finally, and perhaps most significant, culture shock plays a crucial role in the critical dynamic of intercultural—or what Peter Adler calls "transitional"—experience. According to Adler, this dynamic embodies a "positive disintegration" of one's cultural identity in a dialectic of thesis, antithesis, and synthesis. First, the person moves from dependence on traditional identity reinforcements (thesis) through the crisis of culture shock, in which identity is threatened (antithesis), to an independent reaffirmation of self (synthesis)—and, in terms of the culture-learning continuum, from monoculturalism to multiculturalism (Adler 1975).

The dialectic may seem somewhat abstract until you consider these seven ways in which culture shock can contribute to personal growth (Adler 1977):

1. The new situation demands a response. Those responses are built upon a person's making changes in him- or herself. That process of change leads to learning and growth.

2. Strong feelings can be provocative and energizing, especially if the individual tries to understand the origin of the feelings.

3. If levels of anxiety are low, people put up with it. A strong case of culture shock and high anxiety serves as a trigger to do something about the problem.

4. Culture shock is likely to force the individual to learn about other people and their world, why things are the way they are. That is culture learning.

5. New ideas lead to experimentation with behaviors. You try something out and, if it works, you've gained a new coping skill.

6. Culture shock has to do with a sense of contrasts between cultures. As one works through the problems, one can eventually make a fresh confrontation with one's own culture, coming to terms in a new way with one's cultural roots.

7. One's own cultural identity may be threatened, but the experience opens up new avenues of self-realization and self-affirmation.

Overcoming the negative aspects of culture shock

There is no cultural aspirin, though talk is a good antidote to homesickness. Talk with people who are experiencing it at the same time you are, but don't let the discussion degenerate into mere griping. Name your cucarachas, but then explore ways to overcome them productively. Try also to find a willing ear in someone who has been through the cross-cultural adaptation process in the past. Here are some questions to ask:

- What are the paramount needs you have when experiencing culture shock? What do you long for most?
- What triggers culture shock or your homesickness?
- When do you feel the loneliest, the most down?
- Have you had the experience before?
- How do you get over it?

One of the problems in dealing with homesickness and/ or culture shock is that frequently people don't realize (or they deny) they are experiencing it. The feelings are ascribed to other causes. It is difficult to counteract something you don't believe is affecting you, but once you do recognize what is happening, there are a number of things you can do.

1. Find people to interact with. Give them a smile or a little gift. Ask them questions. As you take an interest in them, your feelings will have a focal point outside of yourself.

2. Surround yourself with some familiar things—a favorite jacket, a photo, a cassette. Make your near environment pleasant and reinforcing.

3. Slow down. Simplify your daily tasks. Relax. Let your emotions catch up with the newness all about you.

4. Develop patterns. Follow the same routine each day so that you get a sense of returning to the familiar.

5. Cry. Laugh. Sing. Pray. Draw a picture. Give expression to your feelings.

6. Revise your goals to accommodate a detour instead of scolding yourself for failures.

7. Give new energy to language study, and use it on simple occasions. It is amazing what language success can do for you.

8. Find times and places to get physical exercise.

9. Confide to friends, and even your host family, that you are sad. Their support will warm you.

10. Make a few small decisions and carry them out. Again, your resolve in small things will pay big confidence dividends.

Be assured that, however stressful, culture shock passes if you are willing to let the process of culture learning and cross-cultural adaptation take its course.

Guide 8

Identifying American Value Orientations

"Research into values cannot be value-free," wrote Geert H. Hofstede in *Culture's Consequences: International Differences in Work-Related Values* (1984). "This book reflects not only the values of...participants, but between the lines the values of its authors.... I try as best I can to be explicit about my own value system" (287).

Before you embark on the study of values across cultures, it is important to know your personal value system as well as the value system, to the degree that it differs, of the culture that has helped to shape you into the social being you are.

In this guide we will use data from Hofstede's research to help you consider your culture's value. Hofstede identified four value dimensions:

1. power distance: the degree to which people believe that institutional and organizational power should be distributed unequally

2. uncertainty avoidance: the degree to which people feel threatened by ambiguity and try to clarify uncertainties by establishing new structures

3. individualism: the degree to which people rely upon and have allegiance to the self

4. masculinity: the degree to which people esteem assertiveness, acquisition of wealth, performance, achievement, and ambition (Hofstede's choice of the word "masculinity" was unfortunate since it raises and confuses gender issues)

In his report he describes the "connotations" of each value dimension. A few of these descriptions are reproduced here.

In high power-distance countries

- Parents put high value on children's obedience.

- Students put high value on conformity.

- Managers are seen as making decisions autocratically and paternalistically.

- Employees fear to disagree with their boss.

In high uncertainty-avoidance countries

- There is more emotional resistance to change.

- People fear failure and take fewer risks.

- Hierarchical structures of organizations are expected to be clear and respected; employees prefer clear requirements and instructions.

- There is suspicion toward foreigners as managers, and fewer people are prepared to live abroad.

In high individualism countries

- An employee maintains emotional independence from the company.

- More importance is attached to freedom and challenge in jobs.

- Students consider it socially acceptable to pursue their own goals without considering what others need.
- Individual decisions are considered better than group decisions.
- Individual initiative is socially encouraged.

In high masculinity countries

- The independent decision maker is honored.
- Students aspire to recognition, admire the strong.
- Achievement is defined in terms of recognition and wealth.
- The interference of work in private life is accepted.
- There is higher job stress.
- Managers are relatively less attracted by service roles.

You should be able to define readily the contrasting characteristics of the countries which are "low" in each dimension by moving toward the other end of the continuum. In a low power-distance country, for example, parents put less value on children's obedience (see the first item on the list).

Hofstede compared forty countries in regard to the four values. By asking a variety of questions of 116,000 respondents he was able to come up with a score and a ranking for each country in each value dimension. In your search to locate your own value orientation, it is instructive to see the relative position of the United States in these results. Now that you have a general idea of the four value dimensions, where do you suppose the United States ranks on each—low, middle, or high—among the forty countries? Take a guess. Write down your rankings. Why did you choose those rankings?

Now take a look at the Hofstede figures—01 is high, 40 is low.

The ranking of forty countries in regard to four value systems

Country	Power-Distance Index	Uncertainty-Avoidance Index	Individualism Index	Masculinity Index
Argentina	25	10	23	19
Australia	29	27	02	14
Austria	40	19	18	02
Belgium	12	03	08	20
Brazil	07	16	25	23
Canada	27	31	05	21
Chile	16	10	33	34
Colombia	10	14	39	11
Denmark	38	39	09	37
Finland	33	24	17	35
France	09	10	11	29
Great Britain	31	36	03	09
Germany	31	21	15	09
Greece	17	01	27	17
Hong Kong	09	38	32	17
India	04	34	21	19
Iran	19	24	24	29
Ireland	36	36	12	07
Israel	39	13	19	25
Italy	23	17	07	05
Japan	22	04	23	01
Mexico	03	12	29	06
Netherlands	28	26	05	38
Norway	35	28	13	39
New Zealand	37	30	06	15
Pakistan	21	19	38	22
Peru	14	06	37	31
Philippines	01	33	28	11
Portugal	16	02	31	33
South Africa	25	30	16	12
Singapore	06	40	35	24
Spain	20	10	20	31
Sweden	35	38	11	40
Switzerland	32	25	14	05
Taiwan	19	20	36	27
Thailand	14	22	35	32
Turkey	11	11	26	27
USA	26	32	01	13
Venezuela	03	16	40	03
Yugoslavia	05	05	31	36

The results can be made a little more visual on a bar graph. The four scores of the United States are shown below.

**The ranking of the United States
in regard to four value dimensions**

Index	Power-Distance	Uncertainty-Avoidance Index	Individualism Index	Masculinity Index
high rank (01)			(01)	
(04)			XX	
(08)			XX	
(12)			XX	(13)
(16)			XX	XX
(20)			XX	XX
(24)	(26)		XX	XX
(28)	XX		XX	XX
(32)	XX	(32)	XX	XX
(36)	XX	XX	XX	XX
low rank (40)	XX	XX	XX	XX

The United States had the highest score on the Individualism Index, a relatively high score on the Masculinity Index, a middle-range score on the Power-Distance Index, and a relatively low score on the Uncertainty-Avoidance Index.

Are you surprised at these results? Explain your answer. Perhaps you hadn't thought of your own culture in this way. Perhaps you think of yourself as somewhat different from the mainstream.

Clearly the most dramatic results of the Hofstede study concern the Individualism Index. What are the implications of coming from an individualistic culture? To start out, respond to the following statements quoted from a number of experts on the subject. Do you agree? Disagree? How do they compare? Would you like to elaborate on or restate them?

Statement #1 (Peter Andersen)

> People in the United States are individualists for better or worse. We take individualism for granted and are blind to its impact until travel brings us in contact with less individualistic, more collectivistic cultures (1991, 289).

Statement #2 (Edward T. Hall)

> Western man has created chaos by denying that part of his self that integrates while enshrining the parts that fragment experience (1976, 9).

Statement #3 (Robert N. Bellah et al.)

> Individualism lies at the very core of American culture.... Anything that would violate our right to think for ourselves, judge for ourselves, make our own decisions, live our lives as we see fit, is not only morally wrong, it is sacrilegious (1985, 142).

Statement #4 (John C. Condon and Fathi S. Yousef)

> The fusion of individualism and equality is so valued and so basic that many Americans find it most difficult to relate to contrasting values in other cultures where interdependence greatly determines a person's sense of self (1983, 65).

How do you suppose that your own attitudes and behaviors are shaped by individualism? What are the situations most difficult for you to accept "where interdependence greatly determines a person's sense of self"?

Studying Influences
on Values

Where do values come from? How are values shaped? Who or what does the shaping? Values are neither absolute nor eternal. On the contrary, values, like people, are born. They grow up and sometimes become powerful; sometimes they are pale ideals, honored mainly in the breach. Values grow old. Sometimes they die. Values are not fixed.

You were asked in chapter 5 to explore the relationship of values and formative influences such as worldviews. The implication, of course, is that values are made and molded by other cultural elements. Values, in a sense, reflect other lights. Keeping in mind, then, that values are made and molded, we encourage you in this guide to think some more about their origin and development.

To help you in this task we will adapt work done by Sondra Thiederman (1991, 225-31). She identified a series of value contrasts (forty-two of them) and then compared the United States and other cultures in regard to each one. We will select ten from the list to use in this exercise. Later we will give you two assignments, one of which relates to the blank column, "influences." For now, direct your attention in the configuration which follows to the value contrast in italics, and the descriptions Thiedeman gives for U.S. culture and each contrast culture.

	Ten culture contrasts	
values	**culture descriptions**	**influences**
1. *Change versus tradition*		
U.S. culture:	Change is usually good.	_____
Contrast culture:	Change should be resisted unless there is an obvious good to be gained from abandoning tradition.	_____
Your host culture:		_____
2. *Materialism versus spirituality*		
U.S. culture:	Acquiring material wealth is a sign of success.	_____
Contrast culture:	Spiritual growth is more important than amassing wealth. Material possessions can sometimes be a sign of poor spiritual health and can be disruptive of society.	_____
Your host culture:		_____

values	culture descriptions	influences
3. *Rational versus intuitive thinking*		
U.S. culture:	The most productive thinking is linear, cause and effect, and rational in nature; it is based on concrete evidence and facts.	_____
Contrast culture:	Intuitive, creative thinking is most highly valued.	_____
Your host culture:		_____
4. *Youth versus age*		
U.S. culture:	Young people are valued and the elderly discarded.	_____
Contrast culture:	Age is to be respected.	_____
Your host culture:		_____
5. *Independence versus dependence*		
U.S. culture:	It is unhealthy to be dependent on family and the group.	_____
Contrast culture:	It is proper to remain dependent on the family and group into and throughout adulthood.	_____
Your host culture:		_____
6. *Equality versus hierarchy and rank*		
U.S. culture:	Equality is to be honored.	_____
Contrast culture:	Society is better organized if there is rank, status, and hierarchy.	_____
Your host culture:		_____

values	culture descriptions	influences
7. *Boasting versus modesty*		
U.S. culture:	It is appropriate to speak of one's own achievements.	_____
Contrast culture:	It is disruptive of harmony and social balance to praise oneself.	_____
Your host culture:		_____
8. *Informality versus formality*		
U.S. culture:	Informality and casual appearance are signs of warmth and equality.	_____
Contrast culture:	Informality can be intrusive and can result in loss of respect for a superior.	_____
Your host culture:		_____
9. *Direct versus indirect questioning*		
U.S. culture:	Direct questioning is the best way to get information.	_____
Contrast culture:	Direct questioning is rude and insensitive.	_____
Your host culture:		_____
10. *Confrontation versus avoidance*		
U.S. culture:	Interpersonal conflicts should be discussed directly.	_____
Contrast culture:	Interpersonal conflicts should be dealt with indirectly.	_____
Your host culture:		_____

Before moving into the two assignments in this guide, you may wish to respond to Thiederman's descriptions by adding to them, disagreeing with and rewriting them, or by illustrating them. Putting those descriptions into your own words or thinking of specific behaviors to illustrate each one will help you grasp the point she is making—that cultures differ greatly in their value orientations.

Now for the first assignment. For each of those value contrasts, try to describe your host culture. In some cases your host culture may be nearly identical to U.S. culture or possibly similar to the contrast culture. Chances are that your host culture will be slightly different from both. You will probably discover that it's difficult to write the descriptions, partly because you haven't been in the culture long enough to know it, and partly because a few phrases just aren't adequate to cover the many ways that your culture expresses itself. But try, and promise yourself to return to rewrite them after you learn your new culture better.

The second assignment is even more difficult and may turn into an exercise in conjecture, but the exercise will profitably focus your attention on the subject of value formation. To the right of each description of U.S. culture you'll find a blank line. It's an invitation for you to speculate on some of the influences that may have shaped each of those cultural expressions in the United States and your host culture as well as to suggest the kinds of influences that might give rise to the values identified in the hypothetical contrast culture. (Work on a separate sheet of paper if you wish.)

Although the kinds of influences are likely great in number, you may wish to think particularly about the following questions:

1. How do the understandings of your host culture regarding the origins of life affect their values? Does life evolve from something? From what or whom? Is it created ex nihilo (out of nothing)? By whom?

2. How does their view of nature affect what they hold in high regard and how they behave toward those things? More specifically, do they see nature as something to be controlled and used for their benefit, as something to be feared, or as something to be revered and accommodated?

3. Do they see history as something with a beginning, a linear development, and an eventual culmination, or do they see history as an unending series of cycles? How does their view of history influence their values?

4. What is their understanding of the nature of human beings—that they are essentially good? Fallen and sinful? Or neither? Are humans perfectible? How? Do these understandings contribute to the values that they honor?

5. How have specific events in their history, geography, politics, and economics affected what they hold in high esteem or, conversely, what they hold in low esteem?

In using this guide you may be assured that a person, especially a newcomer to a culture, can't answer such questions definitively. Values are too complex for easy labeling. However, the exercise is justified by the agenda you've set for yourself. Your inquiry into your host culture's values may yield more than almost any other kind of investigation you might undertake.

Personal Essays

Intercultural travel, study, and service all contribute wonderful resources for personal essays. This prose form, which may be written in a journal or otherwise transferred to paper (in a letter to a loved one for instance), typically builds upon anecdotal material and is narrated by a persona by the name of "I," who moves through events. "This is what happened to me." Because the action is made vivid by tangible and sensory details, the reader can be there, with the narrator, experiencing it too. The meaning of the events emerges through the narration, providing fresh insights, evoking emotions, and even effecting attitudinal changes. Because the reader participates in the events with the narrator, he or she experiences them more vividly than if they were narrated by a dispassionate third person.

The personal essay is just that—personal. One spills one's gut in this prose form. It takes courage to write a personal essay, and even more courage to allow one's own vulnerability to be published for others to read. Thanks to Bruce Leininger for the following personal essay.

The mountains of Yunan

China. Have you ever thought of going there? Sounds exciting doesn't it? A whole new world to experience. I've been there: traveled, studied, met people, saw lots of countryside. But to be honest, at the time I wasn't too impressed with the grandness of this strange land. "Big deal. So this is China. It's just another place to fail." I had a habit of getting down on myself. "It seems like no matter what I do 'I can't get no satisfaction'." Secretly, I'd hoped that this mystic land of the East would pull me out of the rut I was in and give me a life that I could enjoy.

My hopes began to fade after I'd visited China's greatest monuments. "I've seen Tiananmen Square, the Great Wall, and the Forbidden City, and still I feel my life slipping away." I mustered up "I'm the luckiest guy I know" feelings whenever I could, but the life-quenching fears always won the upper hand. "Oh God, countless customs that I can't even begin to understand or recognize. I hope I don't offend anyone. I know I feel different from any of the other students in this group. We've spent days together in the same train car, but no one seems interested in knowing who I really am. I don't think anyone will ever understand me. My real feelings will only drive people further away. In any case I'm going to sit here and say as little as possible."

But one afternoon, under the clear, bracing skies of Kunming, the creature I'd hidden inside crawled forth. Kunming lies 26 train-hours distant from Chengdu Normal University where my SST unit was based. As the train tunneled through the mountain ranges of Yunan Province, I began to gather a sense of strength and excitement. I grew up in a land of gently rolling hills, so an encounter with these huge, misty forms rising out of the earth sparked a sense of majesty and mystery in me. Their lure became irresistible, breaking through my self-defeating attitudes and whispering to me, "Give up some of your safety. Sometimes you must follow your desire and surrender to situations beyond your control."

After a lonely week of touring Kunming I found myself sitting in the sun on the patio of the Red Peacock Hotel gazing longingly at the mountains in the distance. I imagined myself perched on their crowns or roving along their backs. "Perhaps their boundlessness, their wildness will let me cast my cares aside for a bit and be free...Oh! But when will I go there and how? Hmmm...No car. No bike. No free ride. Hmmm...I've got legs! I'm going now!"

I, equipped only with basic supplies stuffed into the generous pockets of my travel shorts, skipped down the front steps of the hotel and took my first few strides past farms in the Kunming valley. "Those mountains could be miles away. Chances are that an afternoon's walk will bring them no closer. And once I do reach them I might get lost in this giant web of pathways. The train's leaving for Chengdu tomorrow and I could be left behind, lost in a country where I can't even ask for a bathroom. Hmmm...thinking this way will never get me to the mountains. I'll worry about that later."

The footpath I set off on soon became a road that led to a duck farm by a marsh and ended at a low stone dike/walkway that bounded a lake beyond. In the fields to my right a woman, head wrapped in blue cotton, swung her hoe high, sinking the blade into the soil, turning it over for a new crop. Along the lake fishermen tended nets from rickety wooden piers that extended a stone's throw from the dike/walkway. They sat chatting with their backs turned to me. Every few minutes they stirred to lift their square nets. One of them turned and shared a smile with me. His friendliness touched something deep inside me and softened the worried lump in my throat.

An hour later I left the dike and entered a small town. School had just let out and the street was filled with children playing and fighting. After sighting me they let out with a volley of "hellos." Several of them followed me as the road dipped into a tunnel. Their voices echoed around me as I sang back a "hello" in reply. They caught right on and soon we were doing a blues call and response that would have made B. B. King smile. Two boys walked with me for a stretch while we exchanged token phrases in Chinese and English. "You are Chinese. I am American. Have a good day." If I met such friendly people on my return trip, they'd surely guide me back.

After passing through the town I followed a pipeline and a highway for a while. But time after time I was forced to abandon the thoroughfares and weave my way through a mess of footpaths before finding another main path. The last of these brought me to the foot of the mountains I'd longed for.

I bounded up the path that led up the side of a hill. In my haste I blundered into fields and had to retrace my steps. The grade grew steeper as I fit my hiking shoes into the hand-cut steps. My breath was sharp in my chest as I crossed the last piece of farmland and entered the open meadow. I sprinted to the crest and stood there filled with the excitement that had been growing step by step. Across the plain below I could see the places I'd passed on the way. The whole route was clear now that it was behind me.

I lingered for a moment then started back down.

(Leininger 1990)

At the beginning of the event, what is the person's sense of himself? Of others' dispositions toward him? How does his cultural isolation in China mirror the personal sense of isolation he carries within him? Is his personal sense of isolation intensified or ameliorated by being in a foreign culture? In light of his low self-esteem, what is his initial strategy for coping in China?

The mountain ranges of Yunan Province call to him. Why? How does this phenomenon of nature in China connect with his own person and his cultural heritage? What is the influence of nature upon his thoughts and emotions? What is it about the hills that calls him out of himself?

What does he notice during his hike? That is, the journal reveals to us at a second level what he himself did not screen out. What are the particular sights and sounds that entice responses from him?

Of the range of items you have listed, which of them have to do with human connections? Of what does the communication consist? When connections are made across cultures, what are the simple carriers of meaning? To what extent can he participate in this cross-cultural exchange?

What is the function of the height of the mountains and the author's climb up them in the progression of the essay? More specifically, trace the progression from self-centeredness to other-centeredness. And the progression of his spirits? In what part of the narrative does he use the verb *mustered up? Sprinted?*

What might be implied in the second-to-final statement? Answer in geographical terms. Next, try to give your answer cultural content. Finally, answer in terms of the voyage of his persona. How has he changed?

Do you think the final sentence is triumphant or foreboding?

We hope that this journal entry is sufficient to inspire you to get started in your own journal writing.

Guide 11

Studying Institutions

This guide proposes to do two things: (1) to call your attention to the wide range of institutions available for study and (2) to provide a scheme that defines what an institution is and gives you a framework for examining any institution you might select to study.

Institutions

An institution is any agency or organization structured to provide a service or product to a constituency. Some are private, some public. Some are old, solidly built to last for years, others come and go and, at the moment you happen to study them, are likely to be in a state of change. Their size, complexity, and ambiance vary greatly. But they have something in common—they reveal their cultural context.

While some institutions don't even have a front door to knock on, many others welcome visitors and scholars. Identifying the purpose of your visit will usually reward you with a generous welcome.

Here is a generic list of institutions. It is your job to look for suitable examples that are accessible to you and that, in the examination, will further your learning goals.

agriculture: a coffee, banana, cocoa, or palm oil plantation; a dairy, poultry farm, beef ranch; sugar, flower, or nut farm

art: a theater company, community theater, art gallery, museum of art, the national or state orchestra, a professional music ensemble, artists' league, art or textile co-op

retailing: a central market, department store, shopping center, corner grocery, drugstore, bookstore, organization of street hucksters

communications: a radio or TV station, newspaper plant, magazine publisher, advertising agency, movie theater, record/disc distributor

education: a nursery, kindergarten, primary school, middle school, high school, vo-tech school, ag school, college; a textbook supplier

history and archeology: a museum of history, gold or jade museum, archaeological dig, library

government: the presidential house, court building, legislative assembly building, a ministry office, the housing authority, office of tourism, military organization

health and welfare: a hospital, clinic, home for the aged, children's shelter, drug rehabilitation center, detention center, nutrition center

manufacturing: a mineral processor, car-assembly plant, fabrics manufacturer, tire company, foods processor, utility, petroleum refinery, furniture factory

recreation: a central park program, professional athletic team, the national stadium, a private club

religion: a temple, mosque, cathedral, monastery or convent; a parish school, seminary; a church-run community center; a bazaar

A scheme for studying institutions

After you make arrangements to visit an institution, especially if you are going alone or if you are in charge of a small group, you might be anxious: "But what shall I be looking at? How should I spend my time during the visit? What shall I ask questions about?"

Think of an institution as a structure with many interlinking components, each of which varies in function, size, and shape. Although every institution is different, many are made up of the components shown in this wheel. The spokes are used to represent the interrelatedness of the components.

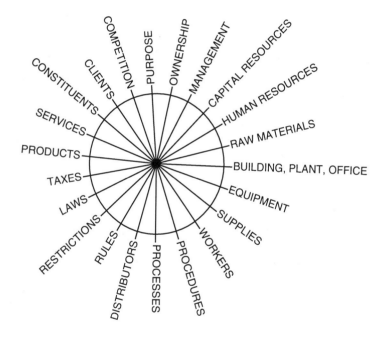

Now that you have in mind a general picture of the many components of an institution, try to describe the institution you are visiting. To do this, use the outline shown on pages 117-118.

To describe the institution's PURPOSE you may have to ask a tour guide, manager, or other informant to explain why the institution was begun and what it hopes to accomplish. Jot down a few of the key words that you hear. Move on to the next component, OWNERSHIP. Is the institution owned by an individual, a partnership, a family, or possibly a number of shareholders? Who are they? Why are they interested in owning the institution? What impact does their ownership have on the product or service? Proceed to the following components.

People typically want to show their institutions in the best light. Allow them to do this. If you have an opportunity, however, try to discover some of the challenges and problems that attend the day-to-day operations. Ask politely about the limitations (such as the capital resources), the restrictions (maybe something having to do with product codes), the odds they have to work against (possibly time or weather or the difficulty of finding good employees). From what you learn, record notes in the outline.

As you become informed about the institution you will discover the linkage among the components. For example, EQUIPMENT and PROCESSES are likely related. So you might ask how changes in equipment (such as computers) have changed the way the institution has done its work. You may assume that DISTRIBUTORS are in some way related to CLIENTS. So your question can anticipate that relationship by asking which of the clients voluntarily come to the institution? Which of them must it find? Which are the hardest ones for the distributors to reach? In such a manner, allow two or more components to inform each other.

components   **your observations and comments**

PURPOSE_____

OWNERSHIP_____

MANAGEMENT _____

CAPITAL RESOURCES _____

HUMAN RESOURCES_____

RAW MATERIALS _____

BUILDING, PLANT, OFFICE _____

components   **your observations and comments**

EQUIPMENT _____

SUPPLIES_____

WORKERS _____

PROCEDURES _____

PROCESSES _____

DISTRIBUTORS _____

RULES _____

RESTRICTIONS _____

LAWS _____

TAXES _____

PRODUCT_____

SERVICES _____

CONSTITUENTS _____

CLIENTS _____

COMPETITION _____

Once you have a pretty good understanding of the institution itself, try to learn about its relationship to the neighborhood, the government, the region, and—you guessed it—the culture.

You may wish to try to answer questions such as these: How do cultural values affect the operation of this institution? For example, is the institution affected by the culture's general preference for affiliation over productivity? Or, how does the culture's authoritarian style show up in this institution? What is the institution contributing to the current social, economic, political, or educational dynamic?

What are/were your expectations when you started your institutional study? Were those expectations based on your knowledge of your own culture, stereotypes of the host culture? How has the institution met or diverged from your expectations? What are the implications of that for the overall process of culture learning in which you are engaged? How are the values and cultural norms of the society reflected in the institution you studied? How might they be improved? How do your criteria for improvement reflect your cultural outlook or the outlook of a knowledgeable host national?

This guide introduced you to the study of institutions in general. The following guide will pertain to a selected institution. After using the two guides, you should have good tools for the study of your institutions of choice.

Studying a Religious Institution

Religion constitutes a central motivation for the people of any culture. Consequently a study of religion can be a profitable unit in your curriculum. This guide suggests three ways you might study religion and elaborates on a selected religious institution: (1) through philosophical inquiry, (2) through a religious ritual or event, and (3) through a religious institution such as a temple, mosque, or church.

Philosophical inquiry

You may want to approach your study of religion with a philosophical frame of mind and think in a slightly more abstract way about worldview, mythos, and religious perception. Your inquiry is likely to be question- and concept-oriented. You will want to use questions such as these:

1. Identify the gods of the culture. Has the concept of God changed or evolved in the past fifty years?

2. Is God transcendent, out beyond, the Holy Other, controlling the universe from a distance; or is God immanent, here and now, inside of humans and an integral part of life?

3. Is the earth considered to be animate—alive with an identity and feelings almost like those of a human, an animal, or a plant?

4. If a child is trampled by a wild animal, do people say that it was the will of God? That it was human error? That it was a matter of chance?

5. Are good health, good fortune, good spirit seen as gifts of God? Is aesthetic beauty attributed to God? Is order considered to be a manifestation of God? Is harmony thought to be rooted in God?

6. Do people curse God? Lay curses upon each other?

7. Do people believe in Satan, devils, or evil spirits? In magic?

8. What would you say the majority of people would consider sacred? Are there sacred places? Sacred objects? Sacred times? Sacred creeds? Sacred people? What endows a place, an object, a time, a creed, or a person with the quality of being sacred?

9. Do the majority of people suppose that an individual has a spirit? A soul? What do people think happens to a human being after death?

10. Are people considered to be basically good but needing discipline or basically bad and needing salvation, or neither good nor bad?

11. When considering the broad subject of knowing, do people think that the deepest knowing comes from personal and disciplined reflection? From hunch? From empirical data? From divine revelation?

12. Is nature considered to be good, bad, or nonmoral? Is God seen as working through nature? Is nature an extension of God? Is God an extension of nature?

Your philosophical inquiry into the cultural meaning of religion can be quickened and informed by myth studies. (This is not myth in the sense of untruth, but myth in the sense of the origin and development of shared meaning.) See chapter 5 again for its reference to people such as Joseph Campbell for whom an understanding of myth is basic to an understanding of life.

Religious ritual or event

While some cultural inquirers know how to use the abstractions of philosophical inquiry, others prefer to use more tangible tools. You might prefer to begin your study of religion by using things you can hear and see, deriving from these experiences a new understanding of the subject.

Among the religious resources you might give attention to are a saint's day, a religious pageant, a festival in a holy week, sacred garb, religious publications, a pilgrimage, religious sanctions, and sacred music.

For example, if you are sojourning in the Moslem world, learning all you can about Ramadan (the fast from sunrise to sunset during the ninth month of the Moslem year) can help you understand Islam. By observing who fasts, how and why they fast, how they behave after sundown (it differs greatly from individual to individual and from culture to culture), and what the effect of the fast is on the society and on individuals, you can extend your appreciation of the power of the Koran, define various kinds or degrees of devotedness, identify crucial markers that distinguish Islamic groups from each other, and understand the reasons for the growth of Islam in the world today.

Religious institution, edifice, or holy place

You may wish to undertake the study using the outline suggested in Guide 11. You can visit a selected church, mosque, synagogue, temple, shrine, or other religious place.

How you organize your study and frame your questions are affected greatly by the religion and the region of your selected institution. If you select a Buddhist temple, for example, the Buddhist monuments in Sanchi in Madhya Pradesh state in India will offer a totally different opportunity for study from the Buddhist pagoda in Ueda, Japan. Buddhism is so complex that you may wish to focus your attention on one aspect, such as on Buddha himself who lived from around 563 to 483 B.C.; the beliefs such as dharma, karma, and pantheism; ethics and morality; rites and restrictions such as dietary laws, death rites, purification rites; or sacred orders of the priesthood or monasticism. In other words, you must tailor your study in a way that uses the resources of the institution well.

Some religious institutions are controlled from a central source (the Roman Catholic Church), while others are local and democratic. You will find synagogues to be of the latter kind. While synagogues typically serve three functions—a house of prayer, a house of assembly, and a house of study—they are essentially democratic institutions, established and maintained by the community of participating Jews. It might include extensive social, recreational, and philanthropic activities and reflect the desires of the local community. Your study of a synagogue, then, is a natural for discovering how a group of people attempt to make their institution culturally appropriate.

The buildings, that is, the structures, are a good place to begin. Be alert to the great contrasts among religions on what a building should look like. A Baha'i temple is constructed to reveal symbolically the spiritual unity of all people. A mosque emphasizes structurally the central place of prayer for the Muslim; its *mihrab* (decorated niche with pointed arch, a place of prayer) faces Mecca toward which prayer is directed. Much of its space, often courtyards, is designed for congregational prayers.

Regardless of what kind of religious institution, edifice, or holy place you select, keep in mind the following six categories of inquiry:

1. The location
2. The structure itself, inside and out
3. Ways that religious meanings are conveyed through architecture, symbols, holy people, art, and tradition
4. Uses to which the edifice or place is put
5. Its care and maintenance
6. The interface of the building or place with its surrounding community, including its religious ministry

We will now illustrate how you can use those six categories of inquiry. Our selected institution is a church of the
Catholic faith. Again we remind you that many of these questions would not be appropriate in studying a Buddhist temple
or, for that matter, the holy places of most other faiths. But
you can see how the questions are framed and how they can
be adapted to your study of a church from another Christian
tradition, a Jewish synagogue, a Hindu shrine, a mosque, a
holy river, cave, or mountain.

1. Examine its exterior. Can you locate works of religious
   art on the walls? What style of architecture is used
   for the building? If there are statues and gargoyles,
   can you identify what symbols are used? Does the
   church face the central square? If so, what other buildings face the square? Is there a public park in proxim-
   ity to the square? Is it in use? Are beggars in sight? If
   so, how are they treated? Is a political event in
   progress? If so, how is it carried out? How do observers respond? Are children free to play in or near the
   sanctuary? Do animals roam in or near the sanctuary? How do people respond to the animals? Do you
   think this is a wealthy or a poor church?

2. Enter the church. Quietly and respectfully examine
   the interior. Locate each of the alcoves from the main
   sanctuary. Attempt to determine the purpose(s) of
   each alcove. Which alcove is dedicated to the church's
   patron saint, the baptistry, the suffering Christ on the
   cross, the Mother Mary with the baby Jesus, the suffering Mary of the crucifixion, etc.? Think about the
   relative size of the various figures and their place-
   ment in the building. Which figures dominate? How
   is God represented? Jesus? The Holy Spirit? Mary?
   Apostles? Angels? Saints? Are all of the figures presented in white skin tones? Is the host culture's heritage reflected in any way? Do you see visible evidence
   of miracles attributed to this church?

3. How is the church being used by the people during
   the time you are present? (If mass is being said, it is
   quite acceptable for you to observe as a non-partici-
   pant. When, during the mass, the peace of God is
   passed, you should greet your neighbor, shake hands,

124

and pass the peace.) Do you notice more men or women in the sanctuary? Are they mostly old people, or young people too? Are priests or nuns in evidence? What specifically religious behaviors do you notice? Is there behavior which surprises you?

4. What type of religious art do you see? Is only one style in use, or is there a mixture of styles? Do any of these works create positive emotions in you? Negative ones? Are any sacred relics on display? To whom/what are they attributed?

5. Sit alone for five to ten minutes. Think about your own religious heritage. How is it similar to Catholicism? Different? How do you think your experience of this church building compares with that of the other persons in the sanctuary?

6. If workers are cleaning or repairing the sanctuary, how does this activity affect those who are worshipping?

7. Leave the church and look again at the exterior art work. How does it fit in with the paintings and sculptures of the interior?

8. Walk through the city blocks which surround the church. What types of homes and businesses are close to the church? Is this a poor town, a middle-class town, or a wealthy one? What criteria are you using to determine class level?

9. Observe public behavior in the vicinity of the church. Do you see any specifically religious behavior?

10. Talk with people in the city. Attempt to find out about the history, the patron saint, the celebrations, miracles, the priests or pastors, the mission, and so forth.

11. What is the relationship of the church to this community? For example, do all bus routes stop near the church? Does the church support hospitals, mission work, parochial schools, or other forms of public service?

12. Who are the priests and other religious workers who serve the needs of this congregation? Are they local people or foreign missionaries? How many priests are

assigned to this parish? For how many persons are they responsible for pastoral care? Do you know how the staff of this church is paid?

13. Identify questions which this study has raised for you—about the church or community, about the role of religion in this community, about the relationship of religion to culture in general, or about your own religion.

Guide 13

A Rock Concert

What is cultural sensitivity? How far should one be expected to go in accommodating other cultures? Case studies may help to define and even answer such questions. The event described in this case study was critical enough so that when I asked one of my students at the end of his three-month term whether there was any unfinished business between him and me, he said, "Yes, I am still angry about not going to that concert!" What was provocative for this student may be provocative for you.

An ethical dilemma

> A big rock concert by Bruce Springsteen and the E Street Band, Peter Gabriel, Sting, Tracy Chapman, and Youssou N'Dour was to be held in the next town. I personally wanted to go, even though as the adult director of our college's study program I might be considered

something of an old fogey. I had thought I might go with my American students as a group, even though the twenty students were to arrive just three days before the concert. But now I had to ask myself this question: Should I refrain from allowing or enabling my group of American students to attend the concert considering the following:

—The stated intent of the concert (to support human rights) is nearly lost to a spreading declamation here that such events encourage moral decadence, including drug consumption.

—An op-ed essay openly doubts that the concert will support true human rights—liberty, respect for life and the dignity of people, equal treatment, conscience in work, the common quest for the public welfare, a spirit of reconciliation, and openness to spiritual values.

—The simple, democratic, and rather religious populace is startled over recent revelations that its terrain is becoming a major transshipment station for cocaine and that apparently some well-placed officials are involved in the activity.

—A local TV sports commentator asks how it is that this country promotes a "Say No to Drugs Day" (September 5) and then follows it the very next week with an activity (the concert) which, in his opinion, says "Yes to Drugs."

—A priest, known for his openness and tolerance, pleads with his parishioners on Sunday to stay away from the stadium, and the archbishop opposes the concert.

—The price of a ticket—$15 (or one thousand colones)—is considered a terrible waste of money in a land where per capita income is considerably less than $2000 a year. (Within the sound of the concert will be people in shack towns, hurting from hunger.)

—The majority of our host families will not permit their own children to attend.

—The event occurs in the first week of the students' visit—the very time of their welding relationships with their families.

—The six-hour concert will end after the buses have stopped running and will greatly complicate the students' getting home.

Should we go and enjoy our music or should we stay home in deference to public opinion and in respect for our hosts?

Questions for discussion

1. What is your opinion of musical performers of this sort? Of their music? Their lyrics? Their lifestyles?

2. What do you know of the human-rights concerts produced internationally by performers such as these in the late 1980s? What did they accomplish?

3. As you read the account above, what are the reasons (explicit or implied) that local people opposed the concert? What are some additional questions that troubled the supplier of this case study?

4. Which of these objections are unique to this one country? Have you heard any of the objections in other parts of the world? Have you heard any of them in your own home community?

5. Which of the objections (by the community or the writer) are, in your judgment, illogical? Based on inadequate information? Prejudiced? Expressions of an exaggerated sensitivity to others? Which objections are reasonable? Based on credible conviction? Derived from documented fact?

6. If you were a member of this student group, just arriving in this country when the concert was being produced, and you were asked to stay away for the reasons mentioned above, what would you do?

7. What principles will you use in resolving conflicts between your personal preferences and your host culture's preferences? Will it make any difference to

129

you if your hosts' standards are more liberal than yours? More conservative than yours?

My Host Father

Here's a case study that gradually emerged in a journal. The writer valued his privacy and was guarded about discussing his personal affairs. He did not like to reveal his feelings to others. Instead, he wrote about his situation in his journal, returning to it many times. The case is presented as an unbroken whole with ellipses indicating the starting and stopping of entries in the journal.

Being male

...in contrast to my host mother's warm welcome, my father was distant tonight. He seemed to speak nothing but soldier-like commands. He told his children to carry my luggage to the room, told his wife to fix food. He even made his younger son get his pipe and tobacco for him.... He doesn't do a stitch in the house. She even puts his food on his plate.... Three out of four nights he's not around. Working, they say. He is apparently a rep for a company in office equipment and computers.... When he talks, I can't understand him, and although I ask him to slow down, he doesn't. He uses idioms and a way of talking quite different from my language teachers and even my host mother.... I'll not forget the day. He said he'd take me to a football (soccer) game. We began by bar hopping, where he was loud and obnoxious and I felt out of place. At bars we picked up his friends and eventually squeezed into the stadium when the game was a quarter over and they were a quarter intoxicated. In the stands, he and his friends became totally offensive. Racial insults. Comments and whistles directed toward women. Most of the stories these guys told were too fast for me to understand. After the game we went somewhere and only after we were in the house did I realize we were with prostitutes. He went into a room with a woman and I remained in a sort of hallway. I didn't know what to do. When he returned we drove home. He didn't say anything and neither did I. This morning at the house, he was again the commander, but didn't seem to recognize me.... I have the impression that he thinks I am effeminate.... By this time I notice how the atmosphere of the house changes when he is around. His children look up to him as a king. They obey him. But I would rather be around my host mother and siblings than with him.... What kind of male is he and what kind of male am I?

Questions for discussion

1. If the guest is accurate in his perceptions, what might be some of the cultural expectations placed upon the male? Which of the behaviors might be more idiosyncratic than cultural?

2. The account does not indicate that the guest noticed any evidence of the father physically abusing his family. Do you think that the family was psychologically hurt by him?

3. From the comments made by the guest, what do you suppose might be some of the cultural influences that color his own point of view? How might his own cultural makeup put him at a disadvantage in this new culture?

4. When looking across cultures, one's perceptions can be distorted. In what ways might the guest's perceptions be faulty, or at least incomplete?

5. Do you think that the guest should have confronted the host father about his outside-the-home conduct? Should the matter have been shared with anyone else?

6. There are cultural observers who'd claim that this picture of a man and his family is not atypical. What is your reaction?

7. Why do you suppose this material remained a private journal topic rather than a matter for group discussion? Do you think it wise to work through this kind of trauma privately? Would he have enhanced its value as a culture-learning experience by talking about it with others?

Guide 15

Reentry Experiences

Cynthia Hockman left her American college campus to spend
time overseas studying and volunteering. Upon her return
she went through reentry shock, an experience that was, at
first, somewhat private. But she got to thinking about it and
decided to talk with other returnees. What she discovered
was the material for a chapbook, later published by
Pinchpenny Press, entitled *Returning Home* (1989). The book
is a type of open microphone in which students tell of their
experiences and feelings upon reentry.

We have adapted several of the statements for this guide.
Although the testimonials might surprise and even astonish
you (does a returnee *really* feel that way?), tuck them in a
corner of your memory. Upon your own return you may wish
to recall some of the statements that express your own feelings.

Returnees remember

Immediate and initial shock: I hated coming back. The first day—getting into Chicago—I didn't even want to be there. I got into the van and I was yelling at the driver to slow down because I thought he was driving too fast. Everything seemed to be flying by. The driver stopped at a Burger King or something and I didn't feel like going in at all.

Things have changed: I was struck by how many things had happened that I didn't know about. I was almost mad in a way—like, "Why didn't you guys tell me?"

Nobody understands: I was angry with my parents and with everybody for not understanding why I was depressed. I just cried at the drop of a hat, and they didn't understand, but I didn't know how to explain to them. They were tired of listening to all my stories. (And I could never make the stories sound the way they really were!) It was frustrating.

I'm homesick...but I'm home: I cried and cried on the plane and on the bus.... I didn't want to come back, and so when I saw my parents, it was nice meeting them, but my mind was still back in my host country.... After a certain point my parents and friends didn't want to hear about it anymore, and I had absolutely no one to talk to.

Some people are so naive: Many people view China as Red China, ideology China, but when I think of China, I think of my students. It makes me mad when people say stuff like, "You couldn't go many places, could you?" or "The KGB watched you, didn't they?" The KGB? This is China, not the Soviet Union.

Am I happy to be an American: Once I got to the U.S., I was repulsed. The grocery store scene was the worst. I walked in and counted over a hundred different kinds of pop and more than that many kinds of breakfast cereal. It made me sick because it just isn't necessary. I was amazed at how much excess we have and how I had never even thought of it as excess.

Life at home bores me: I was sitting around one day after I got home. It was a cold December day. I think it was drizzling. I was so tired of lying around. My overseas travels were such a big adventure and all of a sudden I had no stimulus whatsoever. I had nothing to look forward to except going back to school. I remember getting up, putting on some sweats, and just running. All of a sudden I realized that this was cathartic and I ran as fast as I could— ran and ran and ran.

Why do I feel like this: Part of reentry shock is feeling guilty about my overseas experience—feeling like mine wasn't as good as other people's—and maybe I didn't like it as much as I should have—and maybe I didn't have the best attitude all the time—and feeling like somehow I failed.

Dealing with culture shock, round two

Let's reintroduce Guide 7 as we think further about those testimonials. Review the *stages* of culture shock. At what likely stage were the students when they *reported* on their feelings? When they *experienced* their feelings?

On the basis of the accounts above, list some of the *symptoms* of reentry shock. How are they similar to and different from culture shock?

What do you suppose are the *causes* of reentry shock? Name some situational factors (the home scene), niche factors (not being able to find where you fit in), activity factors (not being engaged yet in significant activities), and self-concept factors (not being able to figure out who you are).

Guide 7 claims that "culture shock is not all bad." Hockman echoes that sentiment: "Many of the uncomfortable feelings associated with return have helped me to expand my world, making me more keenly aware of other cultures. I have learned to be more grateful. The shock I felt when I returned to the United States has helped teach me the value of living not only for myself but for others as well" (39).

Hockman closes her chapbook with specific suggestions for coping with reentry. They're yours for future use:

1. Expect things to be different.
2. Continue to write in your journal.

3. Talk with others who've been overseas and have gone through reentry shock.

4. Talk with a counselor to help you sort through your feelings.

5. Cook a typical meal of your host culture for family or friends.

6. Read the international press.

7. Recognize and get to know people in your home community who are newcomers from overseas. Help them in their adjustment to the United States.

8. Take a course at the local university in international literature, politics, development, art, or ecology.

9. Form or join a discussion group.

What suggestions do you wish to add to Hockman's list? For example, you may wish to include something about keeping in contact with friends in the host culture, preparing an informative photo or journalistic report of the experience to be shared at home, or addressing social and political issues that your international experience has highlighted for you.

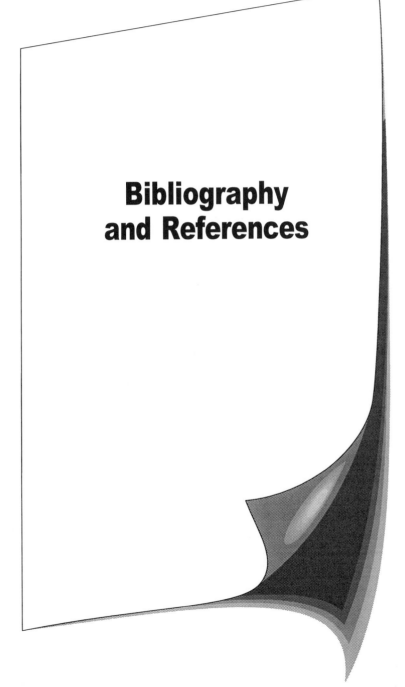

Bibliography
and References

Bibliography
and References

Adler, Peter. "The Boundary Experience—Studies in Human Transformation." PhD diss., Union for Experimenting Colleges and Universities, 1974.

———. "The Transitional Experience: An Alternative View of Culture Shock." *Journal of Humanistic Psychology* 15, no. 4 (1975): 13-23.

———. "Beyond Cultural Identity: Reflections upon Cultural and Multicultural Man." In *Culture Learning: Concepts, Applications, and Research,* edited by Richard W. Brislin. Honolulu: University of Hawaii Press, 1977.

Andersen, Peter. "Explaining Intercultural Differences in Nonverbal Communication." In *Intercultural Communication: A Reader.* 6th ed., edited by Larry A. Samovar and Richard E. Porter. Belmont, CA: Wadsworth, 1991.

Barnlund, Dean C. "Communication in a Global Village." In *Intercultural Communication; A Reader.* 6th ed., edited by Larry A. Samovar and Richard E. Porter. Belmont, CA: Wadsworth, 1991.

Bellah, Robert N., et al. *Habits of the Heart: Individualism and Commitment in American Life.* New York: Harper & Row, 1985.

Bender, David. *American Values, Opposing Viewpoints.* San Diego, CA: Greenhaven Press, 1989.

Bennett, Milton J. "Overcoming the Golden Rule: Sympathy and Empathy." In *Communication Yearbook 3,* edited by D. Nimmo. Philadelphia: International Communication Association, 1979.

――――. "A Developmental Approach to Training for Intercultural Sensitivity." *International Journal of Intercultural Relations* 10, no. 2 (1986): 179-96.

――――. "Towards Ethnorelativism: A Developmental Model of Intercultural Sensitivity." In *Education for the Intercultural Experience,* edited by R. Michael Paige. Yarmouth, ME: Intercultural Press, 1993.

Bochner, Stephen. *The Mediating Person: Bridges between Cultures.* Cambridge, MA: Schenkman, 1981.

Brislin, Richard W., ed. *Cross-Cultural Encounters: Face-to-Face Interaction.* New York: Pergamon Press, 1981.

Broome, Benjamin J. "Building Shared Meaning: Implications of a Relational Approach to Empathy for Teaching Intercultural Communications." *Communication Education* 40 (July 1991): 235-49.

Campbell, Joseph, with Bill Moyers. *The Power of Myth,* edited by Betty Sue Flowers. New York: Doubleday, 1988.

――――. *The Hero's Journey: Joseph Campbell on His Life and Work,* edited by Phil Cousineau. San Francisco: Harper & Row, 1990.

――――. *In All Her Names: Four Explorations of the Feminine Divinity.* San Francisco: Harper, 1991.

Carroll, Raymonde. *Cultural Misunderstandings: The French/American Experience.* Chicago: University of Chicago Press, 1988.

Casse, Pierre. *Training for the Cross-Cultural Mind: A Handbook for Cross-Cultural Trainers and Consultants.* 2d ed. Washington DC: Society for Intercultural Education, Training, and Research, 1981.

Chomsky, Noam. *Language and Mind.* New York: Harcourt, Brace, Jovanovich, 1972.

Condon, John C., and Fathi S. Yousef. *An Introduction to Intercultural Communication.* Indianapolis: Bobbs-Merrill, 1983.

Dodd, Caley H. *Dynamics of Intercultural Communication.* 2d ed. Dubuque, IA: W. C. Brown, 1987.

Eby, Kermit. "Let Your Yea Be Yea." *The Christian Century* 72 (Sept. 14, 1955): 1055-7.

Frost, Robert. "Education by Poetry: A Meditative Monologue." An address given at Amherst College, 1930. In *The Norton Reader: An Anthology of Expository Prose.* New York: Norton, 1973.

Furnham, Adrian, and Stephen Bochner. *Culture Shock: Psychological Reactions to Unfamiliar Environments.* London: Routledge, 1989.

Greene, Theodore Meyer, ed. *Kant Selections.* New York: Charles Scribner, 1929.

Grove, Cornelius L., and Ingemar Torbiörn. "A New Conceptualization of Intercultural Adjustment and the Goals of Training." In *Education for the Intercultural Experience*, edited R. Michael Paige. Yarmouth, ME: Intercultural Press, 1993.

Gudykunst, William B., and Young Yun Kim. *Communicating with Strangers: An Approach to Intercultural Communication.* Reading, MA: Addison-Wesley, 1984a.

————. *Methods for Intercultural Communication Research.* Beverly Hills, CA: Sage, 1984b.

Gullahorn, John Taylor, and Jeanne E. Gullahorn. "Extension of the U-Curve Hypothesis." *Journal of Social Issues* 19 (July 1963): 33-47.

Haglund, Elaine. "Japan: Cultural Considerations." *International Journal of Intercultural Relations* 8 (1984): 61-76.

Hall, Edward T. *The Hidden Dimension.* Garden City, NY: Doubleday, 1966.

———. *Beyond Culture.* Garden City, NY: Doubleday, 1976.

———. *The Silent Language.* Garden City, NY: Doubleday, 1981.

———. *The Dance of Life: The Other Dimension of Time.* Garden City, NY: Doubleday, 1983.

Hall, Edward T., and Mildred Reed Hall. *Understanding Cultural Differences: Germans, French and Americans.* Yarmouth, ME: Intercultural Press, 1990.

Hamilton, Edith. *The Greek Way.* New York: W. W. Norton, 1971.

Hatch, Elvin. *Culture and Morality: The Relativity of Values in Anthropology.* New York: Columbia University Press, 1983.

Herskovits, Melville J. *Cultural Relativism: Perspectives in Cultural Pluralism.* New York: Vintage Books, 1972.

Hofstede, Geert H. *Culture's Consequences: International Differences in Work-Related Values.* Beverly Hills, CA: Sage, 1984.

Hoopes, David S. "Intercultural Communication Concepts and the Psychology of Intercultural Experiences." In *Multicultural Education: A Cross-Cultural Training Approach,* edited by Margaret Pusch. La Grange Park, IL: Intercultural Press, 1979.

InterAct Series. Yarmouth, ME: Intercultural Press, 1984-1997.

Kauffman, Norman L., Judith N. Martin, and Henry D. Weaver, with Judy Weaver. *Students Abroad: Strangers at Home: Education for a Global Society.* Yarmouth, ME: Intercultural Press, 1992.

Kim, Young Yun, and William B. Gudykunst, eds. *Theories in Intercultural Communication.* Newbury Park, CA: Sage, 1988.

Kluckhohn, Florence R., and Fred L. Strodtbeck. *Variations in Value Orientations.* Evanston, IL: Row, Peterson, 1961.

Kochman, Thomas. *Black and White Styles in Conflict.* Chicago: University of Chicago Press, 1981.

Kohls, L. Robert. *Survival Kit for Overseas Living: For Americans Planning to Live and Work Abroad.* 3d ed. Yarmouth,

ME: Intercultural Press, 1996.

Kolakowski, Leszek. *The Presence of Myth,* translated by Adam Czerniawski. Chicago: University of Chicago Press, 1989.

Koller, John M. *The Indian Way.* New York: Macmillan, 1982.

Leed, Eric J. *The Mind of the Traveler: From Gilgamesh to Global Tourism.* New York: Basic Books, 1991.

Leininger, Bruce. Unpublished study journal, 1990.

Lewis, Tom J., and Robert E. Jungman. *On Being Foreign: Culture Shock in Short Fiction, An International Anthology.* Yarmouth, ME: Intercultural Press, 1986.

Luce, Louise F., and Elise C. Smith, eds. *Toward Internationalism: Readings in Cross-Cultural Communication.* Rowley, MA: Newbury House, 1987.

Lustig, Myron W. "Value Differences in Intercultural Communication." In *Intercultural Communication: A Reader.* 5th ed., edited by Larry A. Samovar and Richard E. Porter. Belmont CA: Wadsworth, 1988.

Lysgaard, Sverre. "Adjustment in a Foreign Society: Norwegian Fulbright Grantees Visiting the United States." *International Social Science Bulletin* 7 (1955): 45-51.

Marshall, Terry. *The Whole World Guide to Language Learning.* Yarmouth, ME: Intercultural Press, 1989.

Martin, L. John. "The Contradiction of Cross-Cultural Communication." In *International and Intercultural Communication,* edited by Fisher and Merrill. New York: Hastings, 1976.

Martin, L. John, and Ray E. Hiebert, eds. *Current Issues in International Communication.* New York: Longman, 1990.

Mead Margaret. "Some Cultural Approaches to Communication Problems." In *The Communication of Ideas,* edited by L Bryson. New York: Institute for Religious and Social Studies, 1948.

————. *Sex and Temperament in Three Primitive Societies.* New York: Morrow, 1963.

Oberg, Kalvero. "Culture Shock." Originally presented to the Women's Club of Rio de Janeiro, Brazil, August 3, 1954. Later published as "Culture Shock: The Problem of Adjustment to New Cultural Environments," *Practical Anthropology* 7 (1960): 177-82.

Paglia, Camille. *Sexual Personae: Art and Decadence from Nefertiti to Emily Dickinson*. New York: Vintage Books, 1990.

Paige, R. Michael, ed. *Education for the Intercultural Experience*. Yarmouth, ME: Intercultural Press, 1993.

Rokeach, Milton. *The Open and Closed Mind: Investigations into the Nature of Belief Systems and Personality Systems*. New York: Basic Books, 1960.

———. *Beliefs, Attitudes and Values: A Theory of Organization and Change*. San Francisco: Jossey-Bass, 1968.

———. *The Nature of Human Values*. New York: Free Press, 1973.

———. *The Great American Values Test: Influencing Behavior and Belief through Television*. London: Collier Macmillan, 1984.

Ruben, Brent D. "Human Communication and Cross-Cultural Effectiveness." *International and Intercultural Communication Annual* 4 (December 1977), 98-105. Reprinted in *Intercultural Communication: A Reader*. 5th ed., edited by Larry A. Samovar and Richard E. Porter. Belmont, CA: Wadsworth, 1988.

Samovar, Larry A., and Richard E. Porter, eds. *Intercultural Communication: A Reader*. 5th ed. Belmont, CA: Wadsworth, 1988.

Sarbaugh, Larry E. *Intercultural Communication*. New Brunswick, NJ: Transaction Books, 1988.

Showalter, Stuart W., ed. *The Role of Service-Learning in International Education: Proceedings of a Wingspread Conference*. Goshen College, Goshen IN, 1989.

Sikkema, Mildred, and Agnes Niyekawa. *Design for Cross-Cultural Learning*. Yarmouth, ME: Intercultural Press, 1987.

Singer, Marshall R. *Intercultural Communication: A Perceptual Approach*. Englewood Cliffs, NJ: Prentice Hall, 1987.

Smart, Reginald. "Religion-Caused Complications in Intercultural Communication." In *Intercultural Communication: A Reader.* 5th ed., edited by Larry A. Samovar and Richard E. Porter. Belmont, CA: Wadsworth, 1988.

Spradley, James P., and David W. McCurdy. *The Cultural Experience: Ethnography in Complex Society.* Chicago: Science Research Associates, 1972.

Stewart, Edward C., and Milton J. Bennett. *American Cultural Patterns: A Cross-Cultural Perspective.* Yarmouth, ME: Intercultural Press, 1991.

Storti, Craig. *The Art of Comimg Home.* Yarmouth, ME: Intercultural Press, 1997.

————. *The Art of Crossing Cultures.* Yarmouth, ME: Intercultural Press, 1989.

Thiederman, Sondra. *Bridging Cultural Barriers for Corporate Success: How to Manage the Multicultural Work Force.* Lexington, MA: Lexington Books, D C Heath, 1991.

Triandis, Harry C. "Theoretical Concepts That Are Applicable to the Analysis of Ethnocentrism." In *Applied Cross-Cultural Psychology,* edited by Richard W. Brislin, Newbury Park, CA: Sage, 1990.

Yum, June Ock. "The Impact of Confucianism on Interpersonal relationships and Communication Patterns in East Asia." In *Intercultural Communication: A Reader.* 5th ed., edited by Larry A. Samovar and Richard E. Porter. Belmont, CA: Wadsworth, 1988.